asian bites

asian bites

A feast of flavors from Turkey to India to Japan

Tom Kime

Photography by Lisa Linder

London New York Munich
Melbourne Delhi

Thanks go to my wife, Kylie Burgess Kime, for her ongoing love and support of our great life, and for being such an enthusiastic travel companion. To my mother, Helen, for being the inspiration behind my love of food; to my father, Robert, for igniting my love of travel and discovery; and to my sister, Hannah, for her ongoing curiosity and encouragement to pursue my goals. To my godchildren Frank, Alice, and Raphael, with whom I look forward to sharing many meals. To everyone who loves food and travel.

Project Manager and Editor
Siobhán O'Connor

Managing Editor
Dawn Henderson

Photographic Art Direction and Design
Simon Daley

Senior Art Editor
Susan Downing

Food and Author Photography
Lisa Linder

Editorial Assistant
Ariane Durkin

Food Stylist
Alice Hart

Production Editor
Jenny Woodcock

Prop Stylist
Rachel Jukes

Production Controller
Mandy Inness

First American Edition, 2008
Published in the United States by DK Publishing
375 Hudson Street, New York, New York 10014
08 09 10 11 12   10 9 8 7 6 5 4 3 2 1

JD071—March 2008

Published in Great Britain by Dorling Kindersley Limited

A catalog record for this book is available from the Library of Congress

ISBN: 978-0-7566-3384-4

DK books are available at special discounts when purchased in bulk for sales promotions, premiums, fund-raising, or educational use. For details, contact: DK Publishing Special Markets, 375 Hudson Street, New York, New York 10014 or SpecialSales@dk.com

Color reproduction by MDP, United Kingdom
Printed and bound in China by Leo Paper Group

Discover more at
www.dk.com

Contents

8 Introduction

14 Smoking hot

Seared scallops with fresh chutney | Stir-fried greens with garlic Malaysian fried noodles | Stir-fried bean sprouts with chile bean paste | Marinated grilled mackerel | Chinese barbecue spare ribs Grilled beef patties with shallots and cumin | **Keynotes** Ginger Spicy green beans with chile | Indonesian fried rice | Stir-fried beef with chile and onion relish | Spiced shrimp cakes on sticks of lemongrass | Pork balls with garlic and pepper | Isaan-style grilled chicken | **Keynotes** Soy products | Sardines with green chile sambal | North Vietnamese fish brochettes | Chinese barbecue pork | Garlic and cilantro naan | Sumatran duck sate Marinated barbecue beef

54 Crisp and fiery

Keralan spiced chickpea and lentil dumplings | Fried squid flowers with ginger and spices | Scallion pancakes | Fried puffed potato bread | Turkish zucchini fritters | Crisp peanut wafers | Potato and cauliflower pakoras | **Keynotes** Curry pastes and spice blends Curried sweet corn fritters | Shrimp and chive spring rolls | Spicy lamb-stuffed pancakes | Pork and cabbage dumplings | Sesame tempura | Burmese turmeric fishcakes | Rice flour pancakes Gujarati eggplant fritters | **Keynotes** Chiles | Happy crêpes Sumatran eggplant sambal | Burmese spiced split pea fritters

92 Hot and steamy

Fried bean sprouts and clams | Miso soup with seven-spice chicken
Steamed shrimp wontons | Sichuan chicken dumplings | Steamed
barbecue pork buns | **Keynotes** Rice and noodles | Lamb pilaf with
saffron and nuts | Steamed green vegetable rolls | Mushroom pot-
stickers | Scallion and chive flower rolls | Singapore coconut laksa
Nonya pork, shrimp, and crab ball soup | Nonya-style spicy pork

116 Fresh and aromatic

Sesame chicken salad with white pepper | Chilled seared tuna with
ginger | Citrus dipping sauce | Cured shrimp with shredded lime
leaves | Fresh lettuce cups with chicken | Grilled eggplant salad
Chilled soba noodles with seared salmon | Rena's South Indian
mango pickle | Fresh coconut chutney | Crisp cabbage salad with
peanuts | Nonya bean curd salad | **Keynotes** Coriander, basil, and
mint | Asian salad with pea shoots and sprouts | Pickled daikon
salad with fried garlic | Sashimi of sea bass with hot dressing | Hot
and sour green papaya salad

146 Tangy and refreshing

Malay beef rendang | Sri Lankan smoky eggplant dip | Sichuan spicy
pickled cucumber | Vietnamese peanut dipping sauce | Tamarind
fried shrimp | **Keynotes** Preserved fish products | Roast pork with
fresh mint and peanuts | Spicy apricot chutney | Carrot pachadi

Korean hot pickled cabbage | Spiced stuffed eggplant | Laotian
spice-pickled scallions | Sichuan peppered beef | Lemon and
saffron chicken kebabs | Potato with turmeric and mustard seeds
Keynotes Citrus and lemongrass | Fried eggplant with toasted
sesame seeds | Tomato chutney with green chile | Tamarind
beef with peanuts

182 Sugar and spice

Citrus and young coconut jelly | Yogurt and pistachio cake
Keynotes Nuts and seeds | Persian rice pudding with cardamom
Afghan new year compote | Sour cherry sherbet | Pineapple with
caramelized chile | Elephant ear pastries | Pomegranate and
blood orange fruit salad | Pear fritters with cinnamon honey syrup
Stuffed apricots **Keynotes** Aromatic spices | Mangosteen, lychee,
and mango salad | Yogurt and mint drink | Saffron ice cream
with pistachio nuts

212 Menu ideas

218 Glossary
219 Useful websites
220 Index
224 Acknowledgments

Introduction

It is often said that Asian people are always eating. There seem to be so many opportunities to eat at any time of the day or night. For a chef and a writer that makes Asia an ideal place to travel and sample the wares. Ever present throughout the vastly different countries and cuisines of Asia, with its many hundreds of ethnic groups, is a healthy obsession with food. The constant grazing on freshly cooked ingredients allows visitors to experience a vast wealth of flavors, textures, and taste combinations. These in turn create layers of flavor and three-dimensional tastes that result in food with subtleties, contrasts, and nuances, so that no one ingredient stands out, overpowering the meal.

This same description can be applied to the cultures of Asian countries. Asia is full of blends of

"Asia is full of blends of people, beliefs, and religion, with layers of migration, conquest, and history that work to highlight, complement, and contrast, forming countries with a wealth and depth of heritage."

people, beliefs, and religion, with layers of migration, conquest, and history that work to highlight, complement, and contrast, forming countries with a wealth and depth of heritage. This layering becomes even more interesting because, across the vast continent of Asia, it is impossible to separate the connection of food and society. The styles of food differ enormously from region to region, and the ingredients and recipes change, but the significance of the food remains constant. The food of Asia is an integral part of life. I refer to this as the "anthropology of food," and it makes the connection between food and travel in regions of Asia so enjoyable.

For example, the significance of rice throughout Asia goes much further than as a food staple. How it is cooked is paramount to the success of an Asian meal. Rice is a cultural cornerstone in many ancient heritages that have formed over millennia across a land that covers thousands of miles. The importance of rice lies not only in the food and eating etiquette, but also in the society as a whole: the art, literature, music, religion, spiritual superstitions, economics, and politics of this vast continent. In many Asian cultures, the food that is eaten becomes a meal when eaten alongside rice; without it, the same food would just be a snack. In China, the phrase *chi fan* ("to eat rice") also translates as "to eat." In Thailand and Vietnam, there are scores of phrases that use rice to describe aspects of society, such as generosity, love, and waiting a long time for something to happen—referring to the cultivation of rice. In Thailand, the word for rice is *khao*; a common term of greeting is "*Kin khao laew reu yang*?" ("Have you eaten rice yet?"). Another common greeting in Asia translates roughly as, "Hi, there. You must be hungry." When greeted in this manner, I cannot help but accept the generous offer of more food, even if I have just eaten.

The use of chiles is now synonymous with many Asian cuisines, and it would be hard to imagine the foods of Thailand, India, and Malaysia without this

fiery condiment. Yet it was only after the Portuguese and Spanish had been to South America in the 16th century that Asia embraced chiles in its cuisine. Before the arrival of this heated fruit, however, many of these cuisines were already hot and spicy. Pastes of ginger, garlic, and pepper were used, along with

"It was only after the Portuguese and Spanish had been to South America in the 16th century that Asia adopted the chile into its cuisine. Before the arrival of this heated fruit, many of these cuisines were already hot and spicy. Pastes of ginger, garlic, and pepper were used, along with other spices."

other spices. White pepper was favored in Thai cooking to provide a serious kick. Thai dishes that use white pepper are quite likely to be ancient Siamese recipes predating the Spanish arrival with their hot chiles from South America.

Images of Asia and its varied cuisines are steeped in mystique and intrigue that go back millennia. The sensual delights and aromas of the cuisines of Asia and the Orient evoke ancient trade routes, exotic spice markets, and centuries of secrets that have transfixed everyone who has come into contact with them—including the Romans, who have been documented as using spice blends of cumin and ginger. In Roman cuisine, salty anchovy pastes were used to season dishes in a similar fashion to the way Asian fish sauce and dried and fermented shrimp have been used in Southeast and East Asia for thousands of years.

I am fascinated by the use of spices in Asian cooking, and these extraordinary aromatic seeds and pods from far-distant Asian lands have held outsiders in a spell over many different eras. In England in the 16th and 17th centuries, nutmeg was widely used for both medicinal and culinary reasons because of its taste and strong antibacterial and preservative qualities, but most importantly because it was said to ward off the plague. The Arabs controlled the spice trade, and the spice islands of Indonesia were so valuable that individual sultans amassed great wealth. By the early 1500s, Maluku (or the Moluccas, famous for cloves and nutmeg) was known as Jazirat-al-Muluk, or "Land of Many Kings." Later these islands were crucial in shaping Western history. In the 18th century, at the end of the Second Anglo-Dutch War, the Dutch gained control of Run Island in Indonesia's Moluccan archipelago, and exchanged it for British control of New Amsterdam (Manhattan, New York).

In Asian cooking, the goal is a perfect balance of hot, sweet, salty, and sour tastes. In Thailand, this is called *rot chart*, or "correct taste." This harmony of flavors is achieved through the use of spices, pepper, chiles, fresh herbs, citrus, and salty elements made from fermented and dried soy and seafood products. The wide use of fresh herbs across Asia distinctly marks its cuisines with an aromatic freshness. All these fresh herbs are one of the reasons that Vietnamese food, for instance, is described lovingly as "perfumed" or "fragrant."

In Thailand, they do not restrict themselves to the leaves of fresh coriander (cilantro), but use the roots as well. An analogy is made between a tree with its roots and a bunch of fresh coriander. A tree gains nutrients through its roots; if you translate nutrients into flavor, the roots are where most of the intense flavor is, and the leaves have the least because they are farthest away. Fresh coriander (cilantro) roots are a vital element in the making and flavoring of Thai curry pastes, marinades, and spicy dressings.

This balance of Asian flavors is achieved in all dishes, from the simplest dipping sauce all the way

"Whenever I travel in Asia, I sample so many different dishes of enormous variety, yet I can always trace this simple balance of taste and flavor running through the food."

up to those served at royal banquets. What is unique is that this blend is achieved with strong, pungent, and sharp-tasting ingredients that are overpowering, and even unpleasant, if eaten on their own. Only when paired and blended with other ingredients are these flavors not only tamed, but also perfumed with exotic aromas. The intense fiery heat of spices, pepper, and chiles can be countered with something sweet or neutral such as yogurt or coconut cream, fruits, sugars, honey, roasted root vegetables, or young baby greens, to name but a few. Strong-tasting salty elements such as fish sauce, soy sauce, and other fermented pastes are reined by using sour citrus, lemongrass, lime leaves, or tamarind. Together the elements of hot, sweet, salty, and sour become much more than the sum of their parts. This rule of thumb ensures all the food is harmonious and vibrant. Whenever I travel in Asia, I sample so many different dishes or enormous variety, yet I can always trace this simple balance of taste and flavor running through the food.

The Vietnamese dipping sauce *nuoc cham*, for example, is made by first crushing garlic and salt using a stone mortar and pestle, then adding chopped hot fresh red chiles and pounding them together to make a paste. Fresh lime juice, fish sauce, and a bit of sugar are mixed with the paste. The result is very simple and effective, yet mind-blowingly good. In Thailand, *nam pla prik* is the simplest condiment present on every table—it is nothing more than fish sauce and chopped hot red chiles. When these hot, sour, and salty dressings are served alongside something sweet such as grilled shrimp or beef, fresh crab, or some roasted chicken or pork, the result is astounding because all of your taste buds are stimulated at once. You taste all the elements separately, then together.

Whether preparing a simple sauce or a complex meal, the Asian cook weaves a magic web of taste combinations. These can be hearty and comforting in the first mouthful; delicate and exotic in the next. The food of Asia stimulates all the senses.

The recipes that I have researched in my travels and experiences in Asia are to be enjoyed together. In an authentic Asian meal, numerous courses come to the table in a continual stream, and any number of dishes are eaten together. Unlike Western meals, there is no real separation of dishes or courses. A soup may be eaten alongside a curry or relish, and used to moisten the rice accompanying the meal. The recipes that follow work very well when served in combination with one another. The book's title, *Asian Bites*, signifies bite-sized pieces that can be enjoyed on their own or as part of a larger selection. However you choose to serve them—as snacks, as canapés, as light meals, or as part of sumptuous feasts—it's a great way to bring an evocative taste of the Asian table to yours.

Smoking hot

Charcoal braziers, smoky grills and barbecues, the sizzle of a hot wok—all bring to mind fast food but good food. Whether it is spicy grilled fish, skewers of marinated meat, or an exotic vegetable stir-fry, you will find something to tempt you here. Grilling and barbecuing are an art form in many parts of Asia, where cooking outside is often the norm and all kinds of street food are available. And, of course, there is the fine art of stir-frying—a way to bring fresh, crisp vegetables and succulent meat or seafood to the table in a tasty flash.

Patta kaah ju chatni | Seared scallops with fresh chutney

The flavors and textures of the vivid green chutney combine with sweet seared scallops and roasted nuts to make the layered dimensions of this dish complete. Substitute peanuts or shredded coconut in place of cashews, if you like. Different fresh herbs can also be used, while lemon juice or tamarind pulp could provide the sourness. If you can't find scallop shells, serve the seared scallops on small plates.

Serves 6

For the chutney

4 tablespoons raw cashews

1 garlic clove

½ teaspoon salt

1 teaspoon sugar

4 medium-hot fresh green chiles, seeded and finely chopped

1 large bunch of fresh cilantro, stems and leaves roughly chopped

1 tablespoon Greek-style yogurt

juice of 2 limes

For the scallops

12–18 sea scallops

12–18 scallop shells, cleaned

1¾in (4cm) piece of fresh ginger

2 tablespoons vegetable oil

3 scallions, finely sliced

small handful of fresh cilantro or mint leaves, roughly chopped

salt and freshly ground black pepper

Partner with
Curried sweet corn fritters (pp70–1)
Fresh lettuce cups with chicken (pp124–5)

1 To make the chutney, dry-roast the cashew nuts in a skillet over a medium heat until golden brown; set aside half of the nuts to garnish the scallops. Blend or process the remaining cooled nuts to a paste with the garlic, salt, and sugar. Add the chile and cilantro, and purée. Add the yogurt and 2 tablespoons water, and bring together. Purée until the texture suits your taste; it can be smooth or not. Transfer the fresh chutney to a bowl, and stir in the lime juice. Check the seasoning. It should be hot from the chile; sweet from the nuts and yogurt; and salty and sour from the lime juice.

2 If necessary, remove the small tough muscle from the side of each scallop that attaches the scallop meat to the shell. The orange-colored roe can be left on or removed, to suit your taste. Dry the scallops on paper towels. Finely slice the ginger, then restack the slices and slice into thin shreds like needles. Lightly crush the reserved cashew nuts with the back of a knife.

3 Heat the oil in a large heavy sauté pan over a medium-high heat. Season the scallops with salt and black pepper. Add to the pan. Sear the scallops for 60–80 seconds on each side, depending on their thickness. When the scallops are brown and caramelized on top and bottom, remove to a plate.

4 Place a scallop in each shell. Spoon on a little of the green cashew chutney, sprinkle with some shredded ginger and scallion, followed by some crushed cashew nuts and fresh herbs. Serve immediately. The chutney goes well with other seafood dishes such as fresh crab, grilled shrimp or lobster, or skewers of firm fish.

Rau xanh toi xao | Stir-fried greens with garlic

Like much of Vietnamese food, this dish is simple and delicious. When cooking in a wok, you get an excellent smoky taste to the greens. I had this in Hanoi, where it was made with pumpkin stems, the green curly vines that attach to the pumpkin from the main plant, but any dark, leafy greens will work. Pumpkin, zucchini, or other squash blossoms are also ideal. Try to find pumpkin stems if you can, though, as they are so tasty. I recommend that either you start growing some yourself or you can look for them at farmers' markets or Italian or other specialty produce markets, where they can occasionally be found. These are also good places to look for pumpkin and squash blossoms. Or try your local pumpkin grower if you have one nearby.

1 If using pumpkin stems, peel off the stringy outside fibers, as you would with celery, and cut the stems into 3in (8cm) lengths. Bring a pot of lightly salted water to the boil. Set up a large bowl of ice water nearby. Blanch the greens and zucchini for 3 minutes—they should still have some bite. Strain the vegetables. Immediately plunge the vegetables into the ice water so they stop cooking and retain their bright colors. Strain through a colander.

2 Heat the oil in a wok or pan until hot. Add the garlic and stir-fry for 1–2 minutes until golden. Add the blanched greens and zucchini, and stir-fry for just long enough to coat in the oil and garlic. Season with salt and lots of black pepper. Add the fish sauce and lemon juice, and stir-fry for another 30 seconds. Serve immediately as part of a meal with meat, fish, or rice.

Serves 4

2¼lb (1kg) pumpkin stems or spinach, Swiss chard, or kale, stemmed and torn

3 baby zucchini, thinly sliced horizontally

vegetable oil for stir-frying

3 small garlic cloves, crushed

2 tablespoons fish sauce such as nuoc nam

juice of 1 lemon

salt and freshly ground black pepper

Partner with
Malay beef rendang (pp148–9)
Indonesian fried rice (p32)
Scallion pancakes (pp60–1)

Mee goreng | Malaysian fried noodles

The spicy chile paste used for these noodles can be doubled in quantity and kept in the refrigerator. A little bit of this fiery condiment goes a long way, depending on your chile tolerance. To make this dish entirely vegetarian, omit the chicken and shrimp, and increase the vegetables and tofu.

Serves 4

For the chile paste

10 large dried chiles

5 shallots, peeled

5 garlic cloves, peeled

1 teaspoon shrimp paste (balacan)

6 tablespoons vegetable oil

5oz (150g) firm silken tofu, cut into 1in (2cm) cubes

2 onions, chopped

2 garlic cloves, finely chopped

10oz (300g) skinless chicken breast, cut into slices

10oz (300g) raw shrimp, peeled and deveined

6 choi sum, Chinese flowering cabbage, or bok choy stems, cut into 1¼in (3cm) lengths

1 teaspoon tomato purée

1 tablespoon dark soy sauce

1lb (450g) fresh thin yellow wheat noodles (mee), cut into short pieces

4 scallions (green onions), finely chopped

8oz (225g) bean sprouts, trimmed and rinsed

juice of ½–1 lime

salt and freshly ground black pepper

lime wedges, to serve

1 To make the chile paste, soak the dried chiles in boiling water for 20 minutes until softened. Seed and finely chop. Using a mortar and pestle, pound the chiles, shallots, and garlic into a paste. Add the shrimp paste and 2 tablespoons water, and work into the paste. Heat 1 tablespoon of the vegetable oil in wok over a medium-high heat, and fry the paste for 3–4 minutes, stirring constantly. Transfer to a bowl and wipe out the wok.

2 Heat the remaining oil until hot, and fry the tofu for 3–4 minutes until golden brown. Remove from the wok with a slotted spoon, and drain on paper towels. Add the onion and garlic to the oil, and stir-fry for 2 minutes until fragrant. Add the chicken and stir-fry for another 2–3 minutes. Next, add the shrimp and the choi sum.

3 Add 1 tablespoon of the chile paste, the tomato purée, ½ cup (125ml) water, and the soy sauce, and bring to a simmer. Add the mee noodles (which are available at Asian stores and Chinese supermarkets), and stir-fry for 3 minutes. Add the scallion and bean sprouts, and return the tofu to the wok. Mix together. Taste, then adjust the seasoning with salt and black pepper, and a little lime juice. The shrimp, chicken, and noodles will be sweet; the chile paste will be hot; the soy sauce and the seasoning will be salty; and the lime juice will be sour. Serve immediately with lime wedges.

Suk ju | Stir-fried bean sprouts with chile bean paste

Quick to make and very tasty, *suk ju* is one of many Korean vegetarian dishes. These dishes are collectively referred to as *namul,* and, when a selection is served together, the result is a fully balanced Korean feast. Kochujang, or chile bean paste, gains its fire factor from chiles, adding to the spiciness of this dish. Look for it in Asian markets.

1 Heat the wok or pan over a medium-high heat—it must be hot before you start to cook. Heat the oil, add the garlic, and stir-fry for 30 seconds until fragrant. Add the bean sprouts, sesame oil, light soy sauce, and kochujang. Cook quickly for 1–2 minutes until the bean sprouts start to wilt.

2 Once the bean sprouts have wilted slightly, season well with salt and black pepper. Add the lime juice and cilantro leaves. Toss together and taste. The dish will be hot, sweet, salty, and sour; the bean sprouts should still have a lot of bite and not be soggy.

3 Serve immediately, as the sprouts will continue to cook from the residual heat. They are also delicious cold, but allow the sprouts to cool as quickly as possible by removing them from the wok as soon as they are cooked.

Serves 4–6 as a side dish

1 tablespoon vegetable oil
for cooking

2 garlic cloves, finely chopped

1½–1¾lbs (750g) bean sprouts,
trimmed and rinsed

1 tablespoon sesame oil

1 tablespoon light soy sauce

2 teaspoons kochujang (Korean
chile bean paste)

juice of 1 lime

handful of fresh cilantro leaves

salt and freshly ground
black pepper

Partner with
Pork and cabbage
dumplings (p75)
Fried squid flowers with ginger
and spices (pp58–9)

Ikan panggang | Marinated grilled mackerel

Fresh mackerel is a delicious and simple fish when cooked quickly on a hot grill. In this recipe it is sliced into thick steaks before cooking, but you can leave the fish whole for grilling—and serving—if you prefer. Mackerel is easy to prepare and cook because of its size. The fantastic marinade here features some of the key ingredients of Indonesian cooking that go toward making the food of this region so distinctive. Turmeric, ginger, lemongrass, and lime are combined with coconut cream to make the hot-and-sour marinade. The heat and sourness cut the fattiness of the mackerel, working to bring out the sweetness of the fish.

Serves 4–6

2 limes, plus extra lime wedges, to serve

5 fresh red chiles, seeded and finely chopped

1 teaspoon salt

2 lemongrass stalks, tough outer layer removed, finely chopped

1¾in (4cm) piece of fresh ginger, finely chopped

5 shallots, finely chopped

7fl oz (200ml) coconut cream

1 teaspoon ground turmeric

4–6 whole mackerel, cleaned and cut into thick steaks

1 Cut the skin and pith from the limes with a sharp knife, exposing the flesh. Discard the rind and pith, and finely chop the flesh.

2 Using a mortar and pestle, start grinding the chile and salt. Add the lemongrass and ginger, and work into a paste. Next, add the shallots, then the diced lime flesh. Add some of the coconut cream to bring the paste together. Transfer the marinade to a wide bowl with the remaining coconut cream. Sprinkle in the ground turmeric and mix together.

3 If cooking the mackerel whole, cut 3 diagonal slits through the skin and down to the bone on both sides of the fish to allow the marinade to penetrate right into the center. Or, marinate the steaks in a shallow dish for 30 minutes, spreading the paste over the fish several times.

4 Heat a barbecue or ridged cast-iron grill pan until hot. Grill the fish for 4–5 minutes on each side until browned and cooked through, basting frequently with the spice marinade. Serve straight away with the extra lime wedges for squeezing over, as a snack or appetizer, or as part of a larger Asian meal.

Partner with
Burmese spiced split pea fritters (pp90–1)
Hot and sour green papaya salad (pp144–5)

Paigu | Chinese barbecue spare ribs

These are easy to make and very tasty. Make sure that you buy plenty of ribs because your guests will find it difficult to stop eating them once they have started. You can make these ribs as hot and spicy as you want.

1 Ask your butcher to cut the spare ribs crosswise into thirds measuring 1¾–2in (4–5cm) in length. Put the spare ribs in a large pot of water and bring to the boil. Reduce the heat, and simmer for 20 minutes. Drain and allow to cool. Cut the ribs between the bones to separate them.

2 Mix together the hoisin sauce, soy sauce, rice wine, sugar, honey, tomato paste, garlic, ginger, and chiles in a large bowl. Add the separated spare ribs, and toss to coat in the marinade. Cover and marinate in the refrigerator for at least 3–5 hours, or overnight if possible.

3 Preheat the oven to 350°F (180°C). Line a baking pan with aluminum foil. Spread out the ribs on the tray, and pour on the marinade. Season well with salt and black pepper. Bake in the oven for 45 minutes, turning once during cooking, until golden to dark brown. Serve with lots of paper napkins for wiping sticky fingers.

Serves 4–6

3¼lbs (1.5kg) Chinese-style pork spare ribs

½ cup (125ml) hoisin sauce

3 tablespoons light soy sauce

3 tablespoons Shaoxing rice wine

1 tablespoon brown sugar

1 tablespoon honey

2 tablespoons tomato paste

4 garlic cloves, finely chopped

2in (3 x 5cm) piece of fresh ginger, finely chopped

2 fresh red chiles, seeded and finely chopped

salt and freshly ground black pepper

Partner with
Shrimp and chive spring rolls (pp72–3)
Mushroom pot-stickers (pp106–7)

Cha bo | Grilled beef patties with shallots and cumin

In Vietnam, these flavorful beef patties are grilled on bamboo skewers over sizzling charcoal braziers. They are often served as part of a festive meal called *bo bay mon*, where seven different courses of beef are served at one sitting.

Serves 4

For the beef patties

3 tablespoons sesame seeds

1 teaspoon ground cumin

1lb (450g) lean ground beef

1 garlic clove, very finely chopped

4 shallots, finely chopped

1 tablespoon fish sauce such as nuoc nam

2 tablespoons coconut cream

½ teaspoon curry powder

½ teaspoon sugar

½ teaspoon salt

freshly ground black pepper

Nuoc cham dipping sauce

3 fresh bird's-eye chiles, seeded and thinly sliced

1 garlic clove, finely chopped

1 tablespoon sugar

¼ cup warm water

juice of 2 limes

4 tablespoons fish sauce such as nuoc nam

1 Soak 8 bamboo skewers in cold water for at least 30 minutes, to prevent them burning. Toast the sesame seeds in a dry frying pan over a medium-high heat for about a minute until golden brown. Add the cumin and cook for a further minute until fragrant. Mix the beef, garlic, shallot, fish sauce, coconut cream, curry powder, sugar, salt, pepper, and toasted sesame seeds and cumin together in a bowl. Season with black pepper. Cover and leave to rest in the refrigerator for 20–30 minutes.

2 To make the nuoc cham dipping sauce, using a mortar and pestle, crush two-thirds of the chile with the garlic and sugar until smooth. Add the warm water, then transfer to a bowl, and add the lime juice and fish sauce. Stir to dissolve the sugar. Set aside.

3 Heat a ridged cast-iron grill pan or grill until hot. Divide the beef mixture into 16 portions. Shape each portion into a ball, then gently flatten in your palms to form a 1½in (4cm) patty. Thread two patties onto each bamboo skewer. Grill the beef patties in the pan or over a hot fire for 3 minutes on each side. Do not overcook them, or they will dry out—the beef should be medium-rare in the middle. Quickly sprinkle the remaining chile into the *nuoc cham* dipping sauce (which is hot, salty, and sour), and serve at the table alongside the beef patties for dipping.

Partner with
Spicy green beans with chile (pp30–1)
Isaan-style grilled chicken (pp40–1)

Keynotes | **Ginger**

This tropical rhizome has been used in many forms across Asia for centuries. Ginger (*Zingiber officinale*) has extraordinary culinary and medicinal value, and it would impossible to cook Asian food without it. Every part of the ginger stem can be utilized, imparting an exhilarating spiciness to salads or seafood dishes. The flesh can be pounded, and the juice squeezed from the pulp to be added to dressings and soups. The remaining pulp becomes a staple ingredient in countless curry pastes, or provides the base for many cooked dishes. The skin is used to flavor stocks, broths, braises, and poaching liquids. Ginger can also cut richness, when it is paired with. for example, coconut cream, pork, or roasted duck.

Ginger

Turmeric

Galangal

Balancing flavors

Ginger plays an essential role in the balance of Asian cooking. It can be part of a larger group of flavors with other herbs and spices, or take more of a lead role in the flavor of a dish. When eaten on its own, ginger is hot and peppery, and you would think too overpowering to go with milder elements, but when blended with other ingredients its chameleon-like properties come to the fore. It partners well with chile, with garlic, and with the sour elements of lemon, lemongrass, lime juice, and lime leaves favored in Southeast Asia. The pink-tinged flesh

> "Ginger plays an essential role in the balance of Asian cooking. It can be part of a larger group of flavors with other herbs and spices, or take more of a lead role in the flavor profile of a dish."

of young ginger is delicious pickled in rice vinegar. Known as *gari* in Japan, it is served alongside every portion of sushi the world over. This "baby" ginger is served in syrup in China, and crystallized for use in confectionery and desserts. Young green ginger flowers are delicious at the beginning of the season. They can be stir-fried, imparting their ginger essence and the crisp texture of asparagus. A wild ginger, or *gra chai*, is used in salads, and marinades for curing fish. It has a milder, earthier taste and wetter texture.

Good medicine

Across Asia, ginger is widely used for its medicinal qualities as an antioxidant, its ability to boost the immune system to fight colds and headaches, and to aid digestion. It helps to combat nausea and is also said to counter many of the bacteria that cause sickness when meat and fish are past their best, which can happen quickly in tropical Asian climates. In the holistic schools of ayurvedic and traditional Chinese medicine, in particular, ginger has an important role because of its digestive properties, among other things.

Galangal

Cousins of the ginger rhizome are also important in Asian cooking. One of these is galangal (*Alpinia* spp.), which has a much more fiery, ineed almost medicinal taste than its counterpart. Galangal is largely used in Thailand and Indonesia as a key ingredient in many curry pastes. It is also often found sliced in soups such as *tom yam*, which translates as "hot and sour." It was not until after the Spanish and Portuguese brought back examples of South America's bountiful natural larder that chiles found their way into Thailand in the late 16th century. For centuries previous, ginger and galangal provided the heat and spiciness that form the basis of Thai cooking.

Turmeric

Bright orange turmeric (*Curcuma domestica*) is used fresh in Southeast Asian and South Indian cooking. It has a clean spicy taste similar to ginger and is highly valued for medicinal uses from China across Southeast Asia to India. It has even found champions in Western circles for its purported anti-cancer properties. In Bali, turmeric is the main ingredient of *jarmu*, a liquid herbal base of medicines used in the region. Turmeric is also famed for its dyeing properties— everything that it touches turns a bright yellow.

Kacang panjang | Spicy green beans with chile

Traditionally yard-long beans, also called snake beans, appear in this dish that is sold at Chinese and Malay hawker stalls in Singapore. Yard-long beans have a slightly tougher texture and more flavor than regular green beans. They are likely to be found only in Chinese and Asian stores. If you have trouble locating them, green beans, snow peas, or asparagus can be substituted. Shrimp paste, often labeled *balacan*, is sold in blocks at Asian markets.

Serves 4

For the spice paste

1 lemongrass stalk, tough outer layer removed, finely chopped

3 slices of fresh ginger, chopped

5 garlic cloves, finely chopped

3 fresh red chiles, seeded and finely chopped

10 shallots, chopped

1 tablespoon shrimp paste (balacan)

8 macadamia nuts, roughly chopped

4 tablespoons vegetable oil

14oz (400g) yard-long beans, chopped into 1¾in (4cm) lengths, or a combination of green beans and asparagus, trimmed and halved

1 tablespoon fish sauce such as nam pla

1 teaspoon sugar

Partner with
Singapore coconut laksa (p112)
Roast pork with fresh mint and peanuts (pp158–9)

1 To make the spice paste, use a mortar and pestle to pound the ginger and lemongrass to a paste. Add the garlic and chile, and continue to work. Finally, add the shallot, shrimp paste, and macadamia nuts, and keep working until you have a smooth paste.

2 Heat a wok over a medium-high heat and add the oil. Stir-fry the spice paste for 4–5 minutes until thick and fragrant. Add the beans, fish sauce, and sugar, and stir-fry for another 4–5 minutes until the beans are tender, but still have a bite. While stir-frying the beans, splash with a little water periodically to create steam, not more than ½ cup (100ml) in all. The beans should be cooked, but not swimming in liquid. Serve immediately.

Nasi goreng | Indonesian fried rice

Nasi goreng is prepared in countless ways throughout Indonesia's archipelago of islands, depending on the availability of ingredients or the cook's inclination. If you have been put off by a bad example, please try this tempting version. Make it plain as here to accompany fish or meat dishes, eggs, or sate, or add pieces of diced chicken or pork, seasonal vegetables, or shrimp and other seafood, as desired. As with any fried rice dish, *nasi goreng* is best when made with cold leftover rice.

Serves 4–6

9oz (250g) mixed fresh mushrooms such as shiitake, white, and oyster mushrooms, chopped

2 garlic cloves, finely chopped

2in (5cm) piece of fresh ginger, peeled and finely chopped

2 fresh red chiles, seeded and finely chopped

5 shallots, finely chopped

2 tablespoons vegetable oil

2 cups (500g) cold cooked rice, such as basmati or jasmine

1 large egg, lightly beaten

1 tablespoon ketjap manis (available from Asian markets)

1 tablespoon light soy sauce

1 bunch of asparagus, cut into 1¼in (3cm) lengths

handful of snow peas, topped and tailed (optional)

4 scallions (green onions), finely chopped

1 bunch of fresh cilantro leaves

2 limes

salt and freshly ground black pepper

1 Preheat the oven to 400°F (200°C). Toss the mushrooms with the garlic, ginger, chile, shallot, and a little of the oil. Season with salt and black pepper. Spread the mixture on a baking pan, and bake in the oven for 20 minutes until the mushrooms and shallot have started to caramelize.

2 Break up the rice with a fork to separate the grains. Lightly coat a non-stick frying pan with a bit of oil. Pour the beaten egg into the frying pan and make a thin omelet. Remove the omelet to a cutting board; once cool enough to handle, roll up and slice into thin shreds. Set aside.

3 Heat a wok over a high heat. Add the remaining oil and baked mushroom mixture, including all the juices from the bottom of the pan. Add the rice, ketjap manis, and light soy sauce, and stir-fry for 2 minutes. Add the asparagus and snow peas, if using. Stir constantly for 4–5 minutes until the rice is heated all the way through and the green vegetables are cooked, but still have a bite.

4 Add the scallion, cilantro, and shredded omelet. Add the juice of ½ lime. Check the seasoning. It should be sweet, rich, and earthy; hot from the chile; and salty from the soy sauce. The lime juice adds a much-needed edge to the richness of the dish. Serve with the remaining lime cut into wedges for squeezing over the rice.

Phat neua | Stir-fried beef with chile and onion relish

The technique of stir-frying was brought to Thailand by the Chinese. Thai stir-fries are usually served with the fiery *nam pla prik* (chopped bird's-eye chiles with fish sauce and a little sugar) rather than soy sauce. You will see this condiment throughout Thailand on every table at any street food stall or café. The *nam prik pow* below is good in any kind of stir-fry or as a condiment on sandwiches.

1 Heat a wok over high heat and add the oil—it will be smoky, so work quickly. Stir-fry a third of the meat, spreading it out around the wok, for 2–3 minutes until browned. Remove from the pan and set aside. Repeat with the rest of the beef, cooking in three batches. Return all the beef to the pan, and reduce the heat to medium.

2 Add the chile and onion relish and the asparagus. Simmer for 2 minutes, then add the scallions. Cook for a minute or so until the vegetables are tender, but still crisp. Add the chile and bean sprouts, stir-fry very briefly, then toss in the cilantro and mint leaves. Sprinkle with the lime juice. Check the seasoning. Serve with rice or noodles as a simple meal, or as a part of a larger selection.

Nam prik pow (chile and onion relish) Preheat the oven to 400°F (200°C). In a bowl, mix together 4 coarsely chopped onions, 4 chopped garlic cloves, 6 seeded and finely chopped red chiles, and 1½ tablespoons vegetable oil. Spread the mixture in a baking pan, then roast in the oven for 15–20 minutes until the onion and garlic are soft and caramelized. Scrape the contents of the pan into a food processor or blender. Add 2 tablespoons brown sugar and 1 teaspoon salt; blend to a paste. Add 2 tablespoons tamarind pulp, 2 tablespoons fish sauce (nam pla), and ½ cup water; blend to a smooth paste. Heat 1½ tablespoons oil in a heavy pan over a medium-high heat. Add the chile and onion paste, reduce the heat, and cook for 20–30 minutes until the excess liquid has cooked away. Add the juice of 1 lime, and mix together. Check the seasoning. Pour into sterilized jars and seal with tight-fitting lids. The relish will keep for up to a month in the refrigerator.

Serves 4

2 tablespoons vegetable oil

1lb (450g) top sirloin or other tender beef, cut into thin strips for stir-frying

3 tablespoons chile and onion relish (see recipe below)

5oz (150g) trimmed asparagus, cut into 1¼in (3cm) lengths

4 scallions (green onions), finely sliced on the diagonal

1 large fresh medium-hot chile, seeded and finely chopped

handful of bean sprouts, trimmed and rinsed

handful of fresh cilantro leaves

20 fresh mint leaves

juice of 1 lime

steamed rice or noodles, to serve

Partner with
North Vietnamese fish brochettes (pp46–7)
Pickled daikon salad with fried garlic (p142)

Chao tom | Spiced shrimp cakes on sticks of lemongrass

Chao tom, a spiced shrimp paste, is often wrapped around a small stick of sugar cane, then grilled or fried, so it looks much like a savory lollipop. The sugar cane caramelizes and gives a delicate sweetness to the shrimp paste. While fresh sugar cane can be found in Latino markets, lemongrass is often more readily available. Use halved lemongrass stalks for the sticks. When heated, the lemongrass imparts its unique perfume throughout the center of the shrimp cakes.

Serves 6

12 lemongrass stalks

2¼lbs (1kg) large raw shrimp, peeled and deveined

2 garlic cloves, finely chopped

1¼in (3cm) piece of fresh ginger, finely chopped

2 fresh jalapeño chiles, seeded and finely chopped

1 large egg white

1 tablespoon fish sauce such as nuoc nam

juice of 1 lime

1 tablespoon rice flour

salt and freshly ground black pepper

1 Trim the root end of the lemongrass, but leave the core, which will hold the stalk together. Cut the stems so that they are about 4–5in (10–12cm) long. (The remaining pieces can be used for another dish.) Remove the tough outer layer of the trimmed stalks, and cut the stalks in half through the core so there are 24 half-stems, held in place by the core. Set aside.

2 Put the shrimp, garlic, ginger, and chile into a food processor. Season well with salt and black pepper. Add the egg white, fish sauce, and rice flour, and blend to combine into a paste. Do not overwork—otherwise the mixture will become tough. Fry a small piece of the mixture, taste it, and adjust the seasoning accordingly. Vietnamese dipping sauces for this sort of snack are often salty and sour; the shrimp meat will be quite sweet.

3 Preheat a ridged cast-iron grill pan over a high heat or heat a barbecue until hot. Roll the shrimp mixture into 24 balls, and press a prepared lemongrass stem into the center of each ball. Mold the paste with the palm of your hand around the stem like a lollipop. Grill the shrimp cakes for about 2 minutes on each side, and serve with a Vietnamese dipping sauce such as the *nuoc cham* on p38.

Partner with
Sumatran eggplant sambal (pp88–9)
Scallion and chive flower rolls (pp110–11)

Nem nuong | Minced pork balls with garlic and pepper

In Vietnam, these pork balls are cooked over sizzling braziers at street stalls. At the end of the day, throngs of people returning home after work stop to buy them, and the stalls do a roaring trade. Most eat one skewer right on the spot, then purchase extra highly flavored pork balls to take home—if they last that long. It is hard to resist delving into the small bag that they come in, as you are bustled along by the crowd.

Serves 6

2 tablespoons skinned
  raw peanuts

1 lb (450g) ground lean pork

½ teaspoon salt

7oz (200g) pork fatback
  (available at a butcher)

1 teaspoon sugar

2 garlic cloves, finely chopped

2 fresh red chiles, seeded and
  finely chopped

1 tablespoon fish sauce such
  as nuoc nam

1 tablespoon crushed black
  peppercorns

small handful of fresh cilantro
  leaves, coarsely chopped

Nuoc cham dipping sauce

1 teaspoon rice vinegar

1 teaspoon sugar

1 fresh red chile, seeded and
  finely chopped

1 garlic clove, finely chopped

juice of 1 lime

2 tablespoons fish sauce such
  as nuoc nam

1 Soak 12 bamboo skewers in cold water for at least 30 minutes to prevent scorching. To make the dipping sauce, bring ¼ cup (60ml) water to the boil with the rice vinegar and sugar, then allow to cool. Mix in the chile, garlic, and lime juice, then stir in the fish sauce. Set aside. Dry-roast the peanuts in a heavy pan over a medium-high heat for 3–4 minutes until golden brown. Remove from the pan. When the nuts are cool, coarsely chop them. Also set aside.

2 Mix the pork with the salt and set aside. Fry the pork fatback in a heavy pan over a medium-high heat for about 10 minutes until crisp. Cut into very thin strips, then cut the strips into small dice. Marinate the strips in the sugar, garlic, chile, fish sauce, and crushed black peppercorns for 5 minutes.

3 Combine the pork and the pork fat, including any marinade, and add the cilantro. Make a small ball of the mixture, fry it in a small skillet, and taste. It should be sweet from the sugar and the fat, hot from the chile and the pepper, and salty from the fish sauce and the salt. Adjust the seasoning accordingly. Remember that the dipping sauce will be salty, hot, and sour.

4 Heat a char-grill or barbecue until very hot. Roll the mixture into small balls, and thread them onto the skewers, allowing three or four per skewer. Grill evenly on both sides for 4–5 minutes until brown on the outside and cooked all the way through. Scatter the skewers with the coarsely chopped peanuts, and serve with the *nuoc cham* dipping sauce.

Kai yaang | Isaan-style grilled chicken

Food from the Isaan region in northeastern Thailand close to Laos is famous for its clean flavors and use of herbs. *Kai yaang* uses a delicious method of rubbing a paste into meat and marinating it, then grilling it very slowly, allowing the flavors to caramelize on the skin. This is often done with half a chicken that is flattened out and grilled, then cleaved into pieces. The method here is a bit more manageable.

1 Using a mortar and pestle, grind the lemongrass with the salt and sugar to make a rough paste. Add the garlic and coriander root or stems; continue to pound. Add the crushed black pepper, and pound until you have a semi-smooth paste. Finally, add the fish sauce and mix until well blended. Rub the chicken pieces thoroughly with the paste, and marinate in the refrigerator for at least 2 hours.

2 Preheat a ridged cast-iron grill pan or charcoal barbecue until medium-hot. The chicken is cooked slowly to impart a smoky flavor and allow the marinade to caramelize. Place the chicken in the pan or on the barbecue where it is not too close to the direct heat. Turn frequently—every 3 minutes or so—to prevent burning. When the chicken has caramelized on the outside and the meat is cooked, serve with the Isaan dipping sauce below.

Naam jaew (Isaan dipping sauce) Using a pair of scissors, cut the tops off 3 large dried chiles, and split the chiles up the middle. Seed. Put the chiles in a bowl, and cover with boiling water. Leave for 30 minutes until softened. Wrap 2 teaspoons kapi (Thai shrimp paste) in some foil. Heat a heavy pan over a medium-high heat, and cook the foil parcel for 5 minutes on each side. This makes the paste aromatic, rather than pungent. Chop the drained soaked chiles very finely. Using a mortar and pestle, pound the chiles with ½ teaspoon salt and ½ teaspoon sugar to form a rough paste. Add 6 finely chopped shallots and 2 finely chopped garlic cloves; continue to pound. Work in the roasted kapi. Add 2 tablespoons tamarind pulp (see p154), 1 tablespoon fish sauce (nam pla), and 2 tablespoons water. You will be left with a thick jam-like sauce known as a *jaew*.

Serves 4–6

4 lemongrass stalks, tough outer layer removed, finely sliced

1 teaspoon salt

1 teaspoon sugar

6 garlic cloves, finely chopped

3 fresh coriander (cilantro) roots or 6 cilantro stems, finely chopped

1 tablespoon crushed black peppercorns

1 tablespoon fish sauce such as nam pla

4 whole chicken breasts, with skin on, each cut into 4 pieces

4 chicken boneless thighs, with skin on, halved

Partner with
Nonya bean curd salad (pp136–7)
Tamarind beef with peanuts (pp180–1)

Keynotes | **Soy products**

It is hard to describe Asian cuisine and culture without mentioning the soybean and the vast variety of by-products that are produced from this one plant. Soy has been treasured in Asia for millennia

Soy has been treasured in Asia for millennia because of its versatility. In China soybeans have been grown for 5,000 years, and their use quickly spread throughout the rest of Asia.

because of its versatility. In China, soybeans have been grown for 5,000 years, and their use quickly spread throughout the rest of Asia.

Eaten as sprouts and also as young green fresh beans (known as *edamame* in Japan), soybeans are used to produce milk, which can then be turned into tofu or bean curd, which is eaten in China, Japan, and Korea, as well as Thailand and Malaysia. Tempeh, a lightly fermented bean curd, has a nutty flavor. There are many other pastes, sauces, and condiments that use fermented soybeans as a base, and to which other flavors can be added. Then there is soy sauce, both light and dark, used to marinate and infuse, and as an essential condiment in many Asian cultures. In Java, a soy sauce called *ketjap manis* is traditionally sweetened with palm sugar and scented with star anise and galangal.

Soy makes an important nutritional contribution where there is little or no dairy in the diet and meat is scarce and expensive. A single acre of land growing soybeans can yield nearly 20 times more protein than the same acre used for raising cattle.

Light and dark soy sauce

The use of this quintessential condiment has been documented in Chinese cooking for centuries. It was originally more textured, but today both light and dark soy sauce are strained of all trace of bean solids. Once used to preserve fresh produce over the winter months, soy sauce is the distilled product of roasted soybeans, flour, and water. These are naturally fermented, then aged.

Light soy sauce is not short on flavor—it is the saltier of the two types. It is good for seafood dishes, vegetables, and light dipping sauces. Dark soy sauce is used much more in Northern China.

Miso

Miso is an essential part of Japanese culture and a cornerstone ingredient in Japanese soups, marinades, spreads, and dressings. It is most commonly used as the base for miso soup— a warm bowl of miso soup is a traditional part of any Japanese breakfast. This paste of fermented soybeans varies in color from pale brown, through red, to dark chocolate brown, depending on whether it is fermented with rice, barley, or wheat. Miso is probably most similar to the original runny Chinese soybean sauce that was introduced to Japan about 1,000 years ago by Chinese Buddhist monks. Miso has a wine-like pungency and combines brilliantly with ginger, sesame, and Japanese soy sauce, to work as an anchor in the Japanese range of tastes.

Aged for longer than light soy, it contains a dark molasses. Despite its dark color, its taste is softer than light soy sauce. Important in the Asian larder, it is used in stews and braises, and with meat such as duck, beef, and venison.

Tamari

In Japan, the use of soy sauce (*shoyu*) can be traced back about 1,000 years, when it was introduced by the Chinese. The fermentation method is the same, but Japanese soy sauce tends to have a sweeter, less salty taste, due to a larger proportion of wheat. Tamari is a rich, dark soy sauce made without wheat and much prized in Japan. Unfortunately, not all tamari sold in the West is of the same high quality as in its native Japan.

Tofu and bean curd

Tofu (Japanese) and *doufu* (Chinese) most likely originated in China during the Han Dynasty (206 BC–AD 220). It is made from yellow soybeans that are soaked, ground, and cooked to form the milk product, which is then solidified and aged. Soft bean curd is called *silken tofu* and often comes packed in water. When the bean curd is deep-fried, the smooth texture transforms into a sponge-like web that is crisp on the outside.

Fresh soybeans

Tofu

Soy sauce

Fermented bean products

Fermented bean curd can be preserved in rice wine, brine, or chiles, to be used in condiments. It can be eaten on its on own or as a condiment, or used in seasoning. Red fermented bean curd is naturally colored by adding red rice and has a thick consistency. It is often combined with chiles to make a hot bean paste. This is used in Sichuan cooking, as well as in Korea, where it is called *kochujang* and originates from the region of Sunchang. In both these cuisines, it forms an important and distinctive flavoring.

Sambal lado mudo | Sardines with green chile sambal

This is a dish that could be made with whole fresh sardines, anchovies, or mackerel—all would work well because they are easy to prepare and quick to cook, not to mention very good for you because of the omega-3 oils. You could also serve this sambal with a piece of seared tuna. Use unripe green tomatoes; if they are not available, choose the least-ripe tomatoes that you can find, even though this is the opposite of what you usually look for. The hot and sour elements of the sambal cut the oiliness of the fish. Ask your fishmonger to clean and scale the fish.

1 Peel the shallots and cut in half; remove the core. Finely slice the shallot. Turn the lime leaves over so that the undersides are facing up. Using a sharp knife, shave off the stems so that the leaves lie flat. Place the leaves on top of each other, and roll them tightly like a cigar. With a fast rolling motion of the knife, finely chop the lime leaves into thin needle-like shreds.

2 To make up the sambal, heat the 2 tablespoons oil in a heavy pan over a medium-high heat. Add the shallot, and stir-fry for 2 minutes until fragrant and translucent. Add the green chile, tomato, lime leaves, sugar, and salt. Stir-fry for 3 minutes, then add the lime juice and remove the pan from the heat.

3 Heat a frying pan or ridged cast-iron grill pan over a medium-high heat, and add a little oil. Season the fish with salt and black pepper. Grill the fish for 3 minutes on each side. Be careful not to overcook them, as this will cause them to dry out and lose their flavor. Serve immediately with the green chile and tomato sambal.

Serves 4

5 shallots

2 kaffir lime leaves

2 tablespoons vegetable oil plus extra for cooking

6 fresh green chiles, seeded and finely chopped

2 unripe green tomatoes, seeded and diced

2 teaspoons sugar

1 teaspoon salt

juice of 2 limes

12–16 fresh sardines, cleaned and scaled

freshly ground black pepper

Partner with
Nonya-style spicy pork (pp114–15)
Asian salad with pea shoots and sprouts (pp140–1)

Cha ca nuong | North Vietnamese fish brochettes

In Hanoi's old city, the famous Cha Ca Street used to hold a number of restaurants all selling this spectacular marinated fish. The most well known is Cha Ca la Vong, said to be 135 years old and now owned by the sixth generation of the founding family. This recipe is one of the simplified street-food versions sold in the eatery's vicinity.

Serves 4–6

1lb (450 g) firm white fish such as monkfish, snapper, or grouper

1 onion

2 garlic cloves, finely chopped

1¼in (4cm) piece of fresh ginger, finely chopped

1 fresh red chile, seeded and finely chopped

1 teaspoon ground turmeric

5 tablespoons vegetable oil

3 tablespoons fish sauce such as nuoc nam

2 tablespoons Shaoxing rice wine (or mirin or sake)

4 scallions (green onions), finely chopped

½ bunch of fresh dill, picked and chopped

salt and freshly ground black pepper

3½ oz (100g) skinned raw peanuts, dry-roasted until golden, then roughly crushed, to garnish

lime wedges, to serve

1 Clean the fish, removing the bones and the skin (you could ask your fishmonger to do this). Cut the flesh into 1¼in (3cm) cubes, and put in a glass or ceramic bowl. Grate the onion using a cheese grater, to form a rough pulp. In a bowl, mix the onion, garlic, ginger, and chile. Add the turmeric, 2 tablespoons of the oil, fish sauce, and rice wine, and stir to combine. Pour over the cubed fish, and let marinate, covered in the refrigerator for 2–3 hours.

2 To make the basting sauce, heat the remaining 3 tablespoons vegetable oil in a pan over a medium-high heat. Add the scallions and dill. Cook for 2 minutes until fragrant. Remove from the heat and allow to infuse.

3 Soak a handful of short bamboo skewers in cold water for at least 30 minutes to avoid scorching. Heat a barbecue or ridged cast-iron grill pan until hot. Skewer the pieces of marinated fish onto the bamboo skewers. Season with salt and black pepper. Grill the brochettes of fish on the hot grill for 2 minutes on each side, basting with the scallion and dill mixture while grilling. When they are cooked, scatter with the crushed peanuts, and serve hot with lime wedges.

Partner with
Sichuan chicken dumplings (p100)
Grilled eggplant salad (pp128–9)

Char siu | Chinese barbecue pork

In Chinese cuisine the pig, with all its delicious by-products, is revered above all other animals. There are many variations of Chinese barbecue pork; some are spicier than others, using five-spice in the marinade. It is simple to make and deliciously tasty, and can be used in salads, noodle dishes, soups, lettuce wraps, stir-fries, and the Steamed Barbecue Pork Buns on p101.

Serves 4–6

2 garlic cloves

1 teaspoon five-spice powder

3 tablespoons light soy sauce

2 tablespoons fermented red bean curd (available from Chinese and Asian markets)

1 tablespoon hoisin sauce

1 tablespoon sugar

3 tablespoons Shaoxing rice wine

1¼lbs (600g) pork shoulder, cut into strips 1¼–1¾in (3–4cm) thick

2 tablespoons runny honey

1 Crush the garlic and mix with the five-spice powder. Combine with the soy sauce, fermented bean curd, hoisin sauce, sugar, and rice wine. Put the pork in a shallow glass or ceramic dish, and cover with the marinade. Marinate in the refrigerator for at least 4 hours, turning a few times to ensure that the meat is well coated.

2 Preheat the oven to 450°F (230°C). Fill a deep baking dish with water, and fit a wire rack over the top. Place the pork directly on the rack. Bake in the oven for 30 minutes, basting the pork with the marinade at least three times during the cooking process. Just before the end of the cooking time, preheat the broiler until very hot.

3 Carefully remove the baking dish from the oven, and brush the pork strips with the honey using a pastry brush. Broil the strips until the pork caramelizes and chars slightly around the edges. Serve hot with rice, or sliced into stir-fries and soups. Alternatively, serve individual portions nestled in small, crisp lettuce leaves, ready to pick up and eat.

Partner with
Steamed green
vegetable rolls (p105)
Nonya pork, shrimp, and
crab ball soup (p113)

Naan | Garlic and cilantro naan

Naan with garlic is very difficult to resist. This tear-shaped flatbread originated in the Middle East, but it was the Punjabis in India who introduced it to the rest of the world. It is traditionally cooked on the sides of a tandoor oven, which produces beautiful puffy results. Naan baked in a conventional oven will be flatter, but still very moreish.

1 Whisk the egg, sugar, yogurt, and milk until smooth. Sift together the flour, pinch of salt, and baking soda. Add the yogurt mixture, and combine to make a soft dough. You may need to add a little water, a teaspoon at a time, if the dough seems too stiff. Knead the dough for 3–4 minutes, then add the oil and continue to knead until all the oil has been absorbed into the dough, and the dough is soft and elastic. Put the dough in a bowl, cover with a clean cloth, and let rest in a warm place (room temperature is fine) for 30 minutes.

2 Preheat the oven to 425°F (220°C). Crush the garlic with a little salt to form a paste. Stir the garlic purée, cayenne, cilantro, and scallions into the softened butter. Season with black pepper.

3 Divide the dough into eight balls. Smear a blob of the herb butter onto each dough ball, then flatten the dough so that it is about ¼in (5mm) thick and the rough shape of a teardrop. Allow the dough pieces to rise for another 5 minutes before baking.

4 Lay two naans on a non-stick baking tray, and bake in the oven for 7 minutes until golden. (If you like, you can have two baking trays going at the same time.) Keep the naan warm while you finish baking the rest. Serve with any combination of Indian, Sri Lankan, or Burmese food.

Makes 8

1 large egg
1 teaspoon sugar
1 tablespoon Greek-style yogurt
½ cup milk
2½ cups all-purpose flour
pinch of salt
½ teaspoon baking soda
2 tablespoons vegetable oil
4 garlic cloves, finely chopped
2 tablespoons softened butter
½ teaspoon cayenne
1 small bunch of fresh cilantro, leaves picked
4 scallions (green onions), finely chopped
freshly ground black pepper

Partner with
Sri Lankan smoky eggplant dip (pp150–1)
Lemon and saffron chicken kebabs (pp172–3)

Sate lilit bebek | Sumatran minced duck sate

The West Sumatran region of Padang is famed for its spicy cuisine. The island's wealth of spices such as cinnamon, pepper, chile, and cumin, as well as turmeric, ginger, galangal, and lemongrass, has been fought over for centuries. These quite unusual sate use minced duck meat or chicken, or a combination of the two.

1 To make the spice paste, use a mortar and pestle, or a spice mill, to grind the turmeric, coriander seeds, black peppercorns, cloves, and nutmeg into a powder. Add the macadamia nuts. Put the ginger and galangal in a food processor and pulse to a paste. Add the shallot, chile, and garlic. Blend together until smooth. Combine the ground spices, palm sugar, and shrimp paste, and add to the food processor with the cilantro. Process to combine. Heat the oil in a saucepan over a medium-high heat. Sauté the spice paste for about 5 minutes until fragrant. Set aside to cool.

2 Put the duck meat in the food processor with the salt and crushed black pepper (you do not have to wash the food processor after making the spice paste). Blend into a smooth paste, remove, and combine with the chicken and the cooled spice mix. Turn the lime leaves over so that the undersides are facing up. Using a sharp knife, shave off the stems so that the leaves lie flat. Place the leaves on top of each other, and roll them tightly like a cigar. With a fast rolling motion of the knife, finely chop the lime leaves into thin needle-like shreds. Combine with the duck mixture and mix together.

3 Remove the tough outer layer of the lemongrass and discard. Cut the stems in half through the middle. Mold 2 tablespoons of the sate mixture tightly around the base end of each lemongrass stem. Grill over a hot barbecue or in a preheated ridged cast-iron grill pan for 2–3 minutes on each side until golden brown. Serve straight away. The meat will be perfumed with the spices and lemongrass that have made the island of Padang so famous. You will definitely get the right reaction from your guests when you serve these.

Serves 6

For the spice paste

1½ teaspoons ground turmeric or ¾in (1½cm) piece dried turmeric

1 tablespoon coriander seeds

½ teaspoon black peppercorns

2 cloves

pinch of grated nutmeg

8 macadamia nuts

1¼in (3cm) piece of fresh ginger, finely chopped

1¼in (3cm) piece of galangal, finely chopped (if not available, double the quantity of ginger)

12 shallots, sliced

3 fresh red chiles, seeded and finely chopped

6 garlic cloves, sliced

2 tablespoons palm sugar

1 teaspoon shrimp paste

handful of cilantro leaves

2 tablespoons vegetable oil

1lb (450g) boneless duck breast, coarsely chopped

1 teaspoon crushed black peppercorns

1 teaspoon salt

¾lb (350g) ground chicken

5 kaffir lime leaves

12–14 lemongrass stems

Bulgogi | Marinated barbecue beef

Bulgogi is an essential part of a Korean meal. Wafer-thin slices of sirloin steak are steeped in a marinade containing Asian pear and sesame oil. The meat is quickly grilled, then served with a number of different dips, condiments such as the traditional kimchee, and vegetable side dishes.

Serves 4

1½lb (750g) sirloin beef with a
  good marbling of internal fat

1 Asian pear

1 onion

3 garlic cloves, finely chopped

pinch of salt

3 tablespoons light soy sauce

2 tablespoons sesame oil

2 teaspoons brown sugar

1 tablespoon rice wine such
  as Shaoxing

freshly ground black pepper

1 Remove any excess fat from the piece of beef. Slice the meat into ¼in (6mm) thick slices, or ask your butcher to do this. Peel and grate the pear; repeat with the onion into the same bowl. Using a mortar and pestle, crush the garlic with a pinch of salt to form a paste. Combine the soy sauce and sesame oil in a bowl. Add the brown sugar and garlic paste, and season with lots of black pepper.

2 Take a handful of the pear and onion pulp, and squeeze the juice into a bowl; discard the pulp. Repeat until you have extracted all the juice. Put the the combined juices, beef, and rice wine in a large bowl. Massage the beef with this acidic liquid for 2 minutes. Pour the marinade ingredients over the meat-rice wine mixture, cover, and marinate in the refrigerator for 3 hours.

3 Heat a large skillet or ridged cast-iron grill pan over a high heat. Drain the beef slices. When the pan is hot, sear the meat for 1 minute on each side. Serve immediately with accompaniments such as spicy kimchee. The beef is sweet, sour, and salty. Serving it with a hot dressing or condiment such as the one used with the sea bass on p143 means that you have a balance of all the main tastes.

Partner with
Korean hot pickled
cabbage (p164)
Fried eggplant with toasted
sesame seeds (p178)

Crisp and fiery

So much of Asian food, from whatever tradition or region it originates, is ideal for communal eating, whether it be a meal around the table with lots of different courses or a casual evening of drinks and canapés. This is not to say that Asian food doesn't also make for great snacks at any time of the day. It does. The problem will be learning to share. The food here ranges from the extremely pick-up-able, such as piping-hot fritters, crisp-battered seafood, and tempting pancakes, to bursts of fire, spice, and heat in sambals, fishcakes, and dumplings.

Vaday | Keralan spiced chickpea and lentil dumplings

Similar in texture to a falafel, these fried dumplings are from Kerala in the south of India. When making them, mold them around your little finger like a doughnut. This ensures that as they are frying the heat gets right into the center of the fritters, so that the outside becomes crispy, while the inside is light and fluffy.

Serves 6

½ cup urad dal (split black lentils or black gram)

1 tablespoon vegetable oil plus extra for deep-frying

2 garlic cloves, finely chopped

2 fresh green chiles, seeded and finely chopped

2 medium onions, finely chopped

10 curry leaves (fresh or dried)

1 cup (10oz) cooked chickpeas, rinsed and drained

1 small bunch of fresh cilantro, leaves picked

¾ cup rice flour

1½ teaspoons garam masala

½ teaspoon curry powder (try making your own or buy the freshest Indian blend you can)

½ teaspoon asafoetida powder

½ teaspoon baking powder

salt and freshly ground black pepper

lime or lemon wedges, to serve

Partner with
Rice flour pancakes (p81)
Carrot pachadi (pp162–3)
Potato with turmeric and mustard seeds (pp174–5)

1 Put the urad dal in a bowl, cover with cold water, and soak for 1–1½ hours. Drain, then cover with a fresh batch of cold water. If the dal still has its black husks, plunge your hands into the water, and rub the dal together to remove them—the action is similar to washing your hands. The husks will rise to the surface. Skim off and discard, drain the dal, and again cover with cold water. Continue the rubbing and skimming process for several changes of water, then drain the dal completely. Don't worry about removing all of the husks—just the majority. (If you buy urad dal that has already had the husks removed, just soak and rinse twice.)

2 Heat the 1 tablespoon oil in a heavy pan over a medium-high heat. Fry the garlic and green chile for 2 minutes until fragrant. Add the onion and curry leaves, and continue to fry for 4–5 minutes until softened. Remove from the heat.

3 Put the drained urad dal, chickpeas, onion mixture, and half the cilantro in a food processor. Work into a paste until almost smooth, but with a little texture. Transfer to a bowl. Add the rice flour, garam masala, curry powder, asafoetida, baking powder, and the remaining cilantro, roughly chopped. Mix together, and season with salt and black pepper. Roll the mixture into small balls about 1½in (3.5cm) in diameter; flatten slightly. Make a hole in the center of each ball with your little finger, so that they are like mini doughnuts.

4 Clip a candy thermometer to the side of a large heavy pot, and heat enough oil for deep-frying to 350°F (180°C). If you do not have a thermometer, test the oil with a little mixture—it should sizzle straight away. Fry the dumplings, in small batches, for 2–3 minutes until golden brown. Serve hot with wedges of lime or lemon.

Fried squid flowers with ginger and spices

Squid, shrimp, and other sweet seafood lend themselves well to being fried with a hot and salty coating. The coating can be as simple as salt and pepper, or salt and chile, or a combination of crushed pepper, dried chile and Sichuan pepper. This recipe differs slightly from the usual method of crusting, then frying, that is often served in Chinese restaurants—it adds another layer of flavors.

Serves 4–6

1lb (450g) squid, cleaned

2in (5cm) piece of fresh ginger, chopped

1 tablespoon Shaoxing rice wine

vegetable oil for deep-frying

2 teaspoons spicy salt and pepper (see below)

fresh coriander leaves, roughly chopped, to garnish

lemon or lime wedges, to garnish

For the spicy salt and pepper

1 tablespoon salt

2 teaspoons ground Sichuan peppercorns

1 teaspoon crushed dried red chile flakes

1 teaspoon five-spice powder

1 To make the spicy salt and pepper, mix the four ingredients together, and dry-roast in a small frying pan over a medium heat for 2–3 minutes until fragrant. Set aside.

2 Rinse the squid, and pat dry with paper towels. Score the inside of the squid with a crisscross pattern, making sure not to slice all the way through. Cut into 1¼in x 2in (3cm x 5cm) pieces. Blanch in a pan of boiling water for 30 seconds. Each piece will curl up, and the crisscross pattern will open out like a flower. Remove with a slotted spoon and refresh in cold water. Remove and once again pat dry with paper towels.

3 Using a mortar and pestle, crush the ginger to a pulp. Take the pulp in your hands and squeeze all the juice into a bowl; discard the pulp. Add the rice wine and squid to the juice, and marinate the squid in the refrigerator for 30 minutes.

4 Fill a wok a quarter full with oil, and heat over a medium-high heat. (To check that the oil is hot enough, fry a piece of bread— it should turn golden in about 15 seconds.) Season the squid with 2 teaspoons spicy salt and pepper. (Keep the rest in a glass jar with a tight-fitting lid for other uses.) Fry the squid for 40 seconds in the hot oil, then remove with a slotted spoon and drain well on paper towels. Serve immediately with the cilantro sprinkled on top and the lemon or lime wedges for squeezing over.

Partner with
Sichuan peppered beef (pp170–1)
Fried eggplant with toasted sesame seeds (p178)

Pa jeon | Spring onion pancakes

As with many fine examples of Asian cooking where the ingredients speak for themselves, this Korean omelet is mouthwateringly simple. This version is vegetarian, but shellfish such as shrimp, mussels, or oysters is often added. It works very well with the ginger and sesame dipping sauce.

1 Combine the three flours in a bowl. Whisk in the eggs, then add water, up to 1 cup, to make a smooth batter that is the texture of heavy cream. Season with the salt and some black pepper. Cut the ginger into thin slices, then restack on the chopping board and finely shred. Add the ginger, scallions, and chile to the batter (if you are using shellfish, it should be added at this point).

2 Heat a skillet or omelet pan over a medium-high heat. Add a couple of tablespoons of vegetable oil and rotate the pan to coat, tipping out any excess oil into a dry cup so that it can be used for the next pancake. Add a small ladleful of the batter to the pan, spreading it out to make a thin pancake about 4in (10cm) in diameter. Cook for about 2 minutes until golden brown on the bottom, then turn over with a spatula and cook for a further 2 minutes. Repeat the process until all the batter has been used. Serve immediately with the ginger and sesame dipping sauce below.

Ginger and sesame dipping sauce Delicious with *pa jeon*, which usually contains scallions or oysters, this dipping sauce can be used as a dressing for a salad or as a dipping sauce with fish and shellfish such as raw oysters, grilled shrimp or scallops, or perhaps some steamed mussels or crab. Using a mortar and pestle, crush 2 garlic cloves with ½ teaspoon dried red chile flakes, ½ teaspoon salt, and ½ teaspoon sugar until smooth. Transfer to a bowl, and add 4 tablespoons light soy sauce, 1 tablespoon rice vinegar, 1 tablespoon sesame oil, and 2 tablespoons vegetable oil. Toast 2 teaspoons sesame seeds in a dry frying pan until golden. While the sesame seeds are still warm, grind to a rough paste using a mortar and pestle; add to the dressing. Check the seasoning.

Serves 4–6

⅓ cup glutinous rice flour

⅓ cup rice flour

⅓ cup all-purpose flour

2 eggs, lightly beaten

1 teaspoon salt

2in (4cm) piece of fresh ginger

8 scallions (green onions), cut into 1¼in (3cm) lengths

1 fresh red chile, seeded and cut into fine slivers

about 2 tablespoons vegetable oil

freshly ground black pepper

ginger and sesame dipping sauce (below), to serve

Partner with
Mushroom pot-stickers (pp106–7)
Cured shrimp with shredded lime leaves (p123)

Aloo puri | Fried puffed potato bread

These Indian *puri* are light and puff up spectacularly, giving everyone the impression that you are a magician in the kitchen. They look much more complicated than they actually are. *Puri* are almost identical to *chapatti*, except that they are deep-fried in hot oil, which is what makes them puff up. The secret to the cooking is to flick hot oil over the surface of the *puri* while the bottom is frying in the oil.

Makes about 30 small puri or 15 large ones

8oz (225g) russet potatoes, peeled and cut into equal-sized pieces

2 teaspoons salt

2¼ cups all-purpose flour

2 tablespoons melted butter

about ¼ cup warm water

vegetable oil for deep-frying

1 Put the potato in a saucepan and cover with plenty of cold water. Add 1 teaspoon of the salt and bring to the boil. Simmer for 10–12 minutes until tender to the point of a knife. Drain, then return the potato to the pan over a low heat for 2–3 minutes, to allow it to dry out slightly. Mash and allow to cool.

2 Sift the flour and the remaining 1 teaspoon salt into a bowl. Add the mashed potato and stir through. Make a slight well in the center, and add the melted butter and the water a little at a time, drawing the mixture together until you have a firm dough. Lightly flour your hands and a clean work surface, and knead the dough thoroughly for 10 minutes until soft and elastic. Cover and allow to stand for 30 minutes. (At this stage you could store the dough in the refrigerator for a few hours if well covered, but you get much better "puffy" results if you leave the dough resting for only 30 minutes.)

3 To make either small or large *puri*, roll the dough into 30 small balls (or 15 for the larger ones), then flatten each one into a circle using your hands. Roll out the discs of dough until they are 2–5mm (⅛–¼in) thick. The diameter will vary according to how many you are making.

4 Heat enough oil for deep-frying until very hot. Add one or two *puri* at a time, depending on their size—do not crowd the pan. Immediately start to flick oil over the top of the dough so that it starts to puff up. When the *puri* is golden brown on the bottom, flick it over for another moment or two, and cook until golden on this side as well. Drain on paper towels. Repeat the process until all the *puri* are cooked. Serve hot with a vegetable curry or similar.

Partner with
Stir-fried beef with chile and onion relish (p33)
Tomato chutney with green chile (p179)

Kabak mücveri | Turkish zucchini fritters

Istanbul is an extraordinary city filled with contrasts. Standing astride the two continents of Asia and Europe brings ingredients, cuisines, and cultures together to magnificent effect. The use of Mediterranean herbs such as mint and dill, and spices such as cayenne pepper and a little cumin, illustrates just that. These fritters are sweet from the zucchini, salty from the cheese, and hot from the spices. When served with freshly squeezed lemon juice, they form an ideal combination of flavors.

Serves 4

1 lb (450g) zucchini

2 tablespoons olive oil

1 large onion, finely chopped

1 garlic clove, finely chopped

½ teaspoon cayenne pepper

½ teaspoon ground cumin

3 eggs

3 tablespoons all-purpose flour

30 fresh mint leaves

3 sprigs of fresh dill, leaves picked

8oz (225g) beyaz peynir (white cheese) or feta, broken into small pieces

salt and freshly ground black pepper

a little vegetable oil

lemon wedges, to serve

1 Cut the zucchini into slices about ½in (1cm) thick. Cut the slices into strips ½in (1cm) wide, then restack the strips and cut the zucchini into ½in (1cm) dice.

2 Heat the olive oil in a heavy pan over a medium-high heat. Add the onion, and sweat for 4 minutes until softened. Push the onion to one side to make a little space in the pan. Add the garlic, cayenne pepper, and ground cumin, and sweat for 1–2 minutes until fragrant, then combine with the onion. Add the diced zucchini and sauté for 2–3 minutes. Season with salt and black pepper. (The cheese is salty, so be careful not to overseason.) Leave to cool.

3 Beat the eggs in a large bowl, then stir in the flour until you have a smooth batter. Tear the fresh herbs into the batter, and mix in the cheese. Fold in the zucchini and onion mixture.

4 Heat enough oil to form a film over the bottom of a frying pan over a medium-high heat. Pour in the batter in half-ladlefuls, to make a few fritters at a time. Cook for about 2 minutes until golden brown, then turn over and cook on the other side for another 2 minutes or so. Drain on paper towels, and serve with lemon wedges for squeezing over the top.

Partner with
Spicy lamb-stuffed pancakes (p74)
Spicy apricot chutney (pp160–1)

Rempeyek kacang | Crisp peanut wafers

In Indonesia, these fantastic spicy fried wafers contain coconut cream, peanuts, and candle nuts. Candle nuts are commonly used in many Indonesian dishes. They are not that easy to come by, so substitute the more commonly available macadamia nuts, which are similar in taste and flavor. The crisps can be eaten on their own or as an accompaniment to rice dishes or to vegetable dishes such as the famous *gado gado*, an Indonesian salad of raw and cooked vegetables with a peanut sauce.

1 Spread the peanuts on a roasting tray, and bake in a preheated oven at 350°F (180°C) for 4–5 minutes until pale golden brown. Set aside to cool.

2 To make the spice paste, using a mortar and pestle, work the garlic, coriander seeds, and salt into a paste. Add the macadamia nuts and the shredded lime leaves, and continue to work. Lastly, add the cilantro leaves, and season with black pepper. Work until the paste is smooth.

3 Sift the two flours and turmeric together in a bowl, then add the coconut cream to make a smooth batter. Add the roasted peanuts, and stir through thoroughly. Taste and season with salt and black pepper if required.

4 Heat a heavy high-sided pan over a medium-high heat, and add the vegetable oil. Test whether the oil is hot enough with a little of the mixture—it should fry and sizzle straight away. Carefully drop a tablespoonful of batter at a time into the hot oil, to form wafers. Cooking in batches, fry the wafers for 2–3 minutes until they are crisp and golden. Drain on paper towels, and serve hot or warm.

Serves 6–8

1⅓ cups skinned raw peanuts
1 cup all-purpose flour
1 cup rice flour
1 teaspoon ground turmeric
1 cup coconut cream
1 cup vegetable oil for deep-frying
salt and freshly ground black pepper

For the spice paste
2 garlic cloves
1 tablespoon coriander seeds
1 teaspoon salt
2 tablespoons macadamia nuts
5 kaffir lime leaves, shredded
small handful of fresh cilantro leaves

Partner with
Indonesian fried rice (p32)
Crisp cabbage salad with peanuts (pp134–5)

Zard choba pakora | Potato and cauliflower pakoras

Pakoras are simple but enticing street food snacks eaten throughout Northern India, Pakistan, Afghanistan, and Central Asia. These fiery treats are addictive, and combine spiciness with salt and the sweetness of the vegetables. Accompanied by lemon or lime wedges, their flavor balance is complete.

1 Mix together the coriander seeds, turmeric, cumin, and chile flakes in a bowl. Combine the flour and about 7fl oz (200ml) water to form a smooth batter. Season with the 2 teaspoons salt and black pepper. Leave to rest for 20 minutes.

2 Meanwhile, scrub the potatoes, put in a pan, and cover well with cold salted water. Bring to the boil, and simmer for 10–12 minutes. Remove from the heat, drain, and allow the potatoes to cool. Blanch the cauliflower in boiling water for 3 minutes until softened slightly, but still with a bite. Drain and allow to cool.

3 Mix the dried spices with the batter and cilantro. When the potatoes have cooled, peel off the skin and cut the flesh into ¼in (4mm) slices. Heat the oil for deep-frying in a large heavy pan until hot. Dip the potato slices into the batter, coating well on both sides, then deep-fry them in the hot oil in small batches. (Do not crowd the pan—otherwise the temperature of the oil will drop too much.) The pakoras will rise to the surface once they are cooked. Drain on paper towels, and repeat the process with the cauliflower florets. Cook until golden brown. Sprinkle the pakoras with salt, and serve hot with lemon or lime wedges, or perhaps a fresh cilantro or coconut chutney (see pp16 and 133).

Serves 4–6

2 teaspoons coarsely ground coriander seeds

1 teaspoon ground turmeric

½ teaspoon ground cumin

½ teaspoon dried red chile flakes

1½ cups gram flour (Indian chickpea flour)

2 teaspoons salt

4 large potatoes, scrubbed but unpeeled

½ head cauliflower, broken into even-sized florets

30 fresh cilantro leaves, roughly chopped

vegetable oil for deep-frying

freshly ground black pepper

lemon or lime wedges, to serve

Partner with
Turkish zucchini fritters (p62)
Fresh coconut chutney (p133)

Keynotes | **Curry pastes and spice blends**

The Tamil word *kari*, meaning "sauce," is said to be the origin of the word "curry." It means different things to different people across the vast continent of Asia. Many curries contain chiles, either fresh or dried; however, it was only after the Portuguese had travelled to South America in the 16th century that chiles were introduced to Southeast and South Asia. Before this, black and white pepper were used to create the heat in dishes, along with ingredients such as raw ginger and garlic.

A burgeoning spice trade

Trade in spices has existed between Europe and the East for many centuries. Cooks in the Roman Empire used to grind black pepper, ginger, and cumin that came in on the silk roads from Asia. In

Spice blends and seasonings

Combinations and special blends of spices are myriad throughout Asia. They are at their best and most fragrant when ground to order from whole spices, then blended. Three particular blends found in Asian cuisine are India's garam masala; five-spice powder, used in China and Vietnam; and Japanese seven-spice, or shichimi togarashi.

India's garam masala is a blend of as many as 15 spices and is used in scores of dishes from curries to chutneys. The word *garam* means "hot," and garam masala is often used instead of chile. It usually features black pepper, cumin, cardamom, cloves, bay leaves, coriander seeds, cinnamon, nutmeg, and mace. Households and

Shichimi togarashi

"Conquest, religion, trade, and the migration of populations over many centuries have ensured that curries have travelled across Asia and beyond. It is the spices and spice combinations that make each curry from each region so unique."

the crusades of the 11th century onward, the European clash with the Arab, Persian, and Middle Eastern cultures intensified, and led to a marked increase in the quantity of spices that could be exported. Conquest, religion, trade, and the migration of populations over many centuries have ensured that curries have traveled across Asia and beyond. It is the spices and spice combinations that make each curry from each region so unique.

spice merchants each have their own special recipes. I highly recommend buying an electric coffee grinder and making your own.

Used in China and Vietnam, five-spice powder has both medicinal and culinary importance. Usually a blend of star anise, cinnamon, cloves, fennel seeds, and Sichuan pepper, its distinctive aroma

Curry leaves

Red curry paste

Garam masala

Green curry paste

Thai curry pastes

In Thailand, chopping, grinding, and pounding fresh herbs and spices to form smooth, pungent pastes are the foundations of curry. These curry pastes are known as *kaeng*. Recipes and categories vary from region to region—sour, hot, dry, forest, mountain, or coastal, as well as yellow and *massaman* (which originated in Persia). Red curry paste, or *kaeng daeng* (red curry) or *kaeng phet* (hot curry), is often used as a spicy base for other curries. Thai green curry paste, or *kaeng kwio waan*, gets its heat from green chiles and can vary in intensity. It is generally more fragrant than red curry paste, using lots of lemongrass, lime leaves, and coriander roots, which are pounded together.

When it comes to cooking, there should be a balance of hot from chile; sweet from coconut cream and palm sugar; sour from lemongrass, lime leaves, fresh lime juice, and tamarind juice; and salty from fish or soy sauce.

conjures up images of vibrant markets and delicious food.

A delicious Japanese blend of seasonings, shichimi togarashi, or Japanese seven-spice, contains dried chile flakes and sansho pepper, which is ground from the dried berries of a Japanese variety of prickly ash. Added to the mix are dried mandarin orange zest, black hemp seeds, white sesame seeds, white poppy seeds, and nori (seaweed) flakes.

Curry leaves

The leaves of the small tree *Murraya koenigii* (native to South and Southeast Asia) are used throughout southern India, Sri Lanka, and northern Thailand, as well as parts of Malaysia and in some Indonesian cooking. Curry leaves are best used fresh, but can be used dried if you cannot find fresh ones. Fresh curry leaves can be bought and stored in the freezer until needed. They impart a nutty, bitter taste to dishes, and smell of curry. Similarly to bay leaves, they are used for their flavor and aroma, but not eaten.

Tod man khao phad | Curried sweet corn fritters

I was in a night market in southern Thailand when I first had these. I bought a bag of them straight from the hot oil and enjoyed eating them as I walked around. Before I knew it the bag was empty and I was in need of more. Almost on cue, a boy from the stall I had visited arrived with a tray, shouting out his wares in a singsong voice; I purchased another bag and continued on my way. They are great made with fresh corn, when the kernels are really sweet and the texture is crunchy.

Serves 4–6

4 ears corn on the cob

4 tablespoons all-purpose flour

4 tablespoons rice flour

2 tablespoons red or green Thai curry paste

1 tablespoon fish sauce such as nam pla

1 tablespoon light soy sauce

2 large eggs

¼ teaspoon salt

4 scallions (green onions), finely chopped

handful of fresh Thai basil leaves or cilantro leaves, roughly chopped

vegetable oil for shallow-frying

freshly ground black pepper

1 With a knife, cut the kernels from the cobs of corn. Don't cut away too much of the lower end of the husk, nearest the core of the cob, as these kernels will be tougher. Put the two flours, curry paste, fish sauce, soy sauce, eggs, and the salt in a large mixing bowl. Season with black pepper. Mix together and add the corn kernels, scallions, and basil or cilantro. If the batter is a little dry, add 1–2 tablespoons water, a little at a time—just enough until the batter is the right consistency.

2 Heat enough oil for shallow-frying in a large heavy pan over a medium-high heat. To test whether the oil is hot enough, drop a little of the batter into the oil—it should sizzle right away. Take a tablespoon of the batter and carefully drop it into the hot oil, using the back of a metal spoon to flatten the batter to form a rough patty or cake. Repeat, cooking in batches of a few at a time, so that the temperature of the oil does not drop. Fry for 2–3 minutes on each side until golden and fragrant. When cooked, remove with a slotted spoon and drain on paper towels to soak up any excess oil.

3 Serve hot or at room temperature, with wedges of lime or a sour dipping sauce made with lime juice or rice vinegar (see p38). There will be a great balance of hot, sweet, and salty, set off and brought into balance by the sourness.

Partner with
Chilled seared tuna with ginger (pp120–1)
Tamarind beef with peanuts (pp180–1)

Chun juan | Shrimp and chive spring rolls

Authentic spring rolls eaten as part of dim sum are fine and delicate. They should be no longer than a man's index finger and about twice as wide. Vary the filling according to what's available, maybe using a mix of seafood such as shrimp, crab, scallop, or crayfish. They could be seasoned with spices and chile, or be more herby.

1 Soak the rice vermicelli in boiling water until softened. Drain off the water, and finely chop the noodles so that they are ½–¾in (1.5cm) long. Combine the shrimp with the noodles, and add the sesame oil, light soy sauce, and lemon juice. Season well with salt and black pepper. Add the chives and scallions. Tear in the mint and cilantro leaves. Mix through.

2 Rice paper wrappers are very brittle, so they must be handled with care. Half-fill a large bowl with warm water. Lay out a clean damp tea towel on a clean work surface. Dip a rice paper wrapper in the warm water, and allow to soften for a few seconds. Gently shake off any excess liquid, then lay out on the cloth. Create a bit of a production line, and work on six or so wrappers at a time. When you have six wrappers laid out, spoon a tablespoon of mixture onto each one, near the bottom of each wrapper, but away from the edge.

3 Fold in the left edge, then the right edge, toward the center, then tightly roll away from you. The roll should be compact and tight, rather like a short cigar about 3in (8cm) long. It is important to roll tightly—otherwise the roll will fall apart or explode during frying. Set the finished roll on a plate or a tray. Continue until all the mixture has been used. The rolls can be assembled in advance and kept under plastic wrap in the refrigerator for up to 4 hours before frying.

4 Heat enough oil for deep-frying in a wok or a deep-sided frying pan over a medium-high heat. Fry the rolls in batches of a few at a time, as they tend to stick to each other at the beginning. Cook for about 4 minutes until golden brown. Drain on paper towels, then serve hot. This recipe is well flavored and juicy; if you want to serve a dipping sauce, the choice is yours.

Makes 16 rolls

4oz (120g) rice vermicelli

½–¾lb (300g) cooked shrimp, peeled and deveined, each cut into 3 pieces

1 tablespoon sesame oil

1 tablespoon light soy sauce

juice of ½ lemon

½ bunch of fresh chives, finely chopped

4 scallions (green onions), finely chopped

30 fresh mint leaves

handful of fresh cilantro leaves

1 packet rice paper wrappers

1½–2 cups vegetable oil for deep-frying

salt and freshly ground black pepper

Partner with
Sesame and ginger vinaigrette (p98)
Steamed barbecue pork buns (p101)

Murtabak | Spicy lamb-stuffed pancakes

The making of this stuffed pancake is one of the great sights at the food stalls of Singapore. *Murtabak* makers spin the dough around until it becomes an almost transparent sheet. Fillings for this savory pastry range from egg and diced onion, through cooked peas and pulses, to this spicy meat version.

Serves 6

For the dough

1¾ cups all-purpose flour

1 teaspoon sugar

½ teaspoon salt

2 tablespoons softened butter

¼ cup milk

¼ cup warm water

For the filling

2 tablespoons oil

2 onions, finely chopped

2 garlic cloves, finely chopped

¾in (2cm) piece of fresh ginger, finely chopped

½ teaspoon ground turmeric

½ teaspoon chile powder

2 teaspoons garam masala

2 tablespoons ground cumin

⅔lb (300g) lean ground lamb

1 fresh green chile, seeded and finely chopped

1 small bunch of fresh cilantro, leaves picked and roughly chopped

3 eggs, beaten

1 tablespoon vegetable oil or melted butter for cooking

salt and freshly ground black pepper

1 Mix the flour, sugar, and salt in a large bowl. Rub in the butter using your fingertips, then mix in the liquid until you have a soft, pliable dough. Turn out onto a lightly floured work surface. Knead for 10 minutes until smooth and elastic. Divide into six balls. Lightly oil a clean bowl and add the dough balls. Rest, covered, for 1 hour.

2 Heat the oil in a heavy pan over a medium-high heat. Gently sweat half the onion for 4–5 minutes until soft. Add the garlic and ginger. Sauté for 1 minute, then add the dried spices. Cook for a further minute until fragrant, to combine the flavors. Add the lamb, and season well with salt and black pepper. Stir-fry for about 5 minutes until the meat is browned. Remove from the heat and transfer to a shallow dish to cool. Once cool, stir in the remaining onion, chile, and cilantro. Check the seasoning. Roughly divide the mixture into six equal portions.

3 To shape, lightly oil a work surface. Take a dough ball and, with the palm of your hand, flatten it out. Using an oiled rolling pin and your fingers, gently stretch out the ball until it is a thin disc about 12in (30cm) in diameter. Brush some beaten egg on the disc, then place a portion of the filling in the center. Fold the sides over, and wrap the *murtabak* neatly, as you would a square parcel.

4 Heat a heavy frying pan or griddle pan over a medium-high heat. Drizzle in a tablespoon of oil or melted butter. Gently transfer a pastry parcel to the pan, and cook for 3–4 minutes on each side until crisp and golden brown. Keep warm while you cook the remaining *murtabak*. If serving a lot of people, cut the *murtabak* into 1¾in (4cm) squares, and serve on a large serving platter.

Goenmande | Pork and cabbage dumplings

Pork, cabbage, and black pepper are combined very effectively in these fried dumplings from Korea. Served with a dipping sauce of vinegar, sesame oil, and garlic, they are a great way to start an Asian meal.

1 To make the dipping sauce, crush the garlic with the salt and sugar to form a smooth paste. Add the vinegar, water, and sesame oil, and mix together. Set aside.

2 Heat the 2 tablespoons oil in a heavy pan over a medium-high heat. Sauté the garlic and ginger for 2 minutes until fragrant. Add the pork and continue to sauté, stirring, for 5 minutes until the meat has browned.

3 Add the shredded cabbage to the pan with the soy sauce, some salt, and some black pepper. Reduce the heat and cover the pan. Braise for about 5 minutes until the cabbage has wilted, but still has a little bite. Taste the pork and cabbage—the mixture should be spicy from the black pepper. Adjust the seasoning if necessary, then remove the pan from the heat and leave to cool. Once cool, add the scallions and mix together.

4 Lay out six wonton wrappers at a time, and place 2 teaspoons pork and cabbage mixture on each wrapper. Brush the edges with a little water, and fold over to make a half-moon. Squeeze the edges tightly closed, using your thumb and finger to press out any air bubbles. Cover with a damp cloth until ready to cook.

5 Heat the oil for shallow-frying in a heavy pan over a medium-high heat. Test the oil to see whether it is hot enough—a crumb of bread should start to sizzle straight away. Fry the dumplings in batches of six at a time so that the oil does not drop in temperature while they are cooking. Drain on paper towels. Serve hot, accompanied by the dipping sauce.

Makes 18

2 tablespoons vegetable oil plus
   ½ cup extra for shallow-frying

2 garlic cloves, finely chopped

1¾in (4cm) piece of fresh ginger,
   finely chopped

1lb (450g) ground pork

½ Chinese cabbage, heart
   removed and leaves shredded

2 tablespoons light soy sauce

4 scallions (green onions), finely
   chopped

18 round wonton wrappers

salt and lots of freshly ground
   black pepper

For the dipping sauce

1 garlic clove

½ teaspoon salt

½ teaspoon sugar

2 tablespoons rice vinegar

2 tablespoons water

2 tablespoons sesame oil

Partner with
Miso soup with seven-
spice chicken (pp96–7)
Sichuan spicy pickled
cucumber (p152)

Iri goma tempura | Sesame tempura

Tempura is made by dipping vegetables and shellfish into a light batter, then quickly frying them. Shellfish and fresh asparagus are particularly good when prepared this way because they remain very tender and still firm inside. This technique can be used with other vegetables, such as onions, zucchini, and broccoli.

Serves 6

vegetable oil for deep-frying

all-purpose flour for dredging

3 soft-shell crabs, cleaned and halved

18 large raw shrimp, peeled but with tails left intact

6 scallions (green onions), trimmed and cut in half

9 thin asparagus spears, cut to the same size as the scallions

salt and freshly ground black pepper

1 recipe *ponzu* (see p122) or other dipping sauce of your choice, to serve

Sesame tempura batter

½ cup cornstarch

scant 1 cup self-rising flour

3 tablespoons sesame seeds

1 teaspoon sea salt

about 1½ cups ice water

Partner with
Marinated barbecue beef
(pp52–3)
Asian salad with pea shoots
and sprouts (pp140–1)

1 To make the tempura batter, put the cornstarch, self-rising flour, sesame seeds, and sea salt in a bowl. Whisk in the ice water, and mix together to form a slightly lumpy batter, rather than a smooth one—tempura batter should have small lumps of dried flour.

2 Half-fill a large high-sided pan with vegetable oil for deep-frying, and heat over a medium-high heat until 180°C (350°F). To check whether the oil is the right temperature, fry a small piece of bread—it should turn golden in about 15 seconds. Season the all-purpose flour with salt and black pepper.

3 Start with the halved soft-shell crabs. Dredge with the seasoned flour, shaking off any excess flour. Dip the crab in the batter. Taking care not to splash the hot oil, lower the crab into the oil, and deep-fry for 3–4 minutes until golden brown, turning once during cooking. Drain on paper towels. Repeat the process with the shrimp. Deep-fry the shrimp for 2 minutes until they are pale golden, cooking them in batches so that the temperature of the oil does not drop. Drain on paper towels. Lastly, batter and deep-fry the scallions and asparagus in the same way. Cook for 1–2 minutes so that they are still crunchy and not overcooked.

4 Serve everyone a selection of each type of tempura. Have either individuals bowls of the *ponzu* dipping sauce (p122) or another dipping sauce alongside each serving, or place one bowl in the center of the table. Remember that the dipping sauce needs to have salty, sour, and hot elements to cut the rich sweetness of the fresh shellfish, scallions, and asparagus.

Ngephe gyaw | Burmese turmeric fishcakes

Burma has a long southern coastline on the Andaman Sea and is rich in all kinds of fish and seafood. These typical fishcakes use a combination of fish and shrimps, but a combination of fish varieties, or fish and shrimps, crab, or squid would be authentic, as the seafood in this region is so plentiful and a large part of the diet. The use of turmeric and ground ginger shows that this is a recipe with origins in India.

Serves 6

1lb (450g) firm white fish such as cod or snapper

1 teaspoon ground ginger

½ teaspoon ground red chile flakes

1 garlic clove

3 shallots

¾lb (350g) raw shrimps, peeled and deveined

handful of fresh cilantro leaves

1 tablespoon fish sauce such as nam pla

1 teaspoon ground turmeric

1 cup vegetable oil

salt and freshly ground black pepper

1 Remove the skin and bones from the fish, and cut into 1¼in (3cm) dice. Put the ginger, chile, garlic, and shallots into a food processor, and pulse to make a coarse pulp. Add the shrimp and fish to the food processor with the cilantro and fish sauce. Continue to work until a smooth paste forms. (Do not add the turmeric at this stage because it will dye the food processor bowl orange.)

2 Transfer the fish paste to a metal bowl. Add the turmeric and mix with your hands until the paste is orange, to ensure the turmeric is evenly combined with the rest of the fish mixture. Season with salt and black pepper. Mix through.

3 Moisten your hands with a little water. Roll the fish mixture into 3in (7cm) sausages about 1in (2.5cm) thick. Heat the vegetable oil in a large pan or wok until hot. Fry a few of the fishcakes, adding one at a time. The fish cakes will expand, so do not add too many to the hot oil at one time. Fry for 4–5 minutes until golden brown, then drain on paper towels. Serve hot with a chile dipping sauce.

Partner with
Grilled beef patties with shallots and cumin (pp26–7)
Pickled daikon salad with fried garlic (p142)

Appam | Rice flour pancakes

Appam are traditionally cooked in a high, round-sided omelet pan called a *kuali*. The thick batter is swirled around the pan so that it forms thin lacy edges. Serve as suggested here, or eat plain to accompany a meal instead of rice. Or try them as a sweet snack, sprinkled with brown sugar and grated fresh coconut or sliced banana.

1 Dissolve the yeast and sugar in the warm water, and leave for 10 minutes until the mixture starts to froth. Meanwhile, put the rice flour and coarser ground rice in a food processor. With the motor running, gradually add half the coconut cream to form a smooth dough. Add the yeast mixture to the dough and mix together, then transfer to a large bowl. Cover the dough and leave to rise in a warm place for 1 hour until it has doubled in size.

2 When the dough has doubled in size, stir the salt into the remaining coconut cream, then mix the coconut cream into the dough to form a batter the thickness of heavy cream. The batter is ready to use, or it can be refrigerated for up to 2 hours until needed.

3 Heat a small omelet pan until quite hot over a medium-high heat. Grease the bottom and sides of the pan with oil, then tip out the excess to be used for the next pancake. Gently drop in a large ladleful of batter and, holding the pan in both hands and using an oven mitt, swirl the batter around so that it rides up and sticks to the sides of the pan. Pour any excess batter back into the bowl. Cover the pan with a lid, and reduce the heat to low to steam the center of the pancake for 1 minute.

4 If you are making the *appam* with fried eggs, crack an egg into the center of the pancake. Season with salt and black pepper, if using, and again cover the pan—this time for 3 minutes. The lacy edges of the *appam* should be golden brown and crisp, and the center of the egg perfectly cooked. Repeat the process with the other pancakes. Serve immediately with some chile relish or sambal (see pp33, 45, and 89). Alternatively, if not using eggs, try one of the suggestions listed above.

Makes 6–8

2 teaspoons fresh yeast

1 teaspoon sugar

½ cup warm water

1¾ cups (200g) rice flour

1¼ cups (200g) ground rice

2 cups coconut milk

½ teaspoon salt

a little vegetable oil for greasing

6–8 eggs (optional)

salt and freshly ground black pepper (optional)

Partner with
Gujarati eggplant fritters (pp82–3)
Tomato chutney with green chile (p179)

Ringrah na bhajia | Gujarati eggplant fritters

Gujarat, in northwestern India, is home to vibrant vegetarian dishes made according to ancient recipes. Chickpeas and pulses are grown and used fresh, and ground into flour that makes noodles, breads, and batters. Make lots of these smoky fritters because everyone will keep coming back for more.

Serves 6–8

3 medium eggplant

1 cup (300g) cooked chickpeas, drained and rinsed (you can use canned chickpeas)

2 tablespoons rice flour

1 tablespoon all-purpose flour

½ teaspoon baking powder

4 scallions (green onions), finely chopped

2 hot fresh green chiles, seeded and finely chopped

3 garlic cloves, finely chopped

1 teaspoon ground cinnamon

½ teaspoon cayenne

handful of fresh cilantro leaves, roughly chopped

2 eggs, lightly beaten

vegetable oil for frying

sea salt and freshly ground black pepper

Spiced yogurt

1 teaspoon ground cumin

1 teaspoon ground coriander

1 cup (8oz) Greek-style yogurt

½ teaspoon cayenne

20 fresh cilantro leaves, roughly chopped

juice of ½ lemon

1 Preheat the broiler. Place the eggplant on a baking sheet under the broiler and char all over until the skin is blistered and the eggplant are soft inside, turning with tongs as necessary. Remove from the broiler and leave to cool. Once the eggplant are cool, peel off the skin and discard. Coarsely chop the flesh and set aside.

2 To make the spiced yogurt, roast the ground coriander and cumin seeds in a dry frying pan for 1–2 minutes until fragrant. Leave to cool, then stir into the yogurt with the cayenne. Season with salt and black pepper. Mix the cilantro with the lemon juice, add to the yogurt mixture, and stir through.

3 Put the drained chickpeas in a large bowl. Roughly mash with the two flours and baking powder. Add the chopped eggplant, scallions, chiles, and garlic, and stir, then add the cinnamon, cayenne, chopped cilantro. Season with salt and black pepper. Lightly beat the eggs and add to the bowl. Using a metal spoon, combine the ingredients into a batter.

4 To cook the fritters, heat a large heavy pan over a medium-high heat and add a couple of tablespoons of vegetable oil. Fry a little piece of the mixture, and taste to check the seasoning. If necessary, adjust the seasoning to suit your taste. Cooking in batches so that you don't crowd the pan and allow the temperature of the oil to drop, carefully spoon tablespoons of batter into the pan. Shallow-fry for 2–3 minutes, turning once during the cooking time, until the fritters are golden brown and cooked through. Drain on paper towels, and serve hot with the spiced yogurt.

Keynotes | **Chiles**

If you were to sum up a cuisine in one word, "hot" could be one of those used for many Asian cuisines. Before the introduction of chile (*Capsicum frutescens*) to Asian food, much of the heat found in dishes came from white pepper and spices such as ginger, galangal, and garlic. In Thai cooking, if you come across a recipe that is made with white pepper, it is often an old Siamese recipe predating the arrival of chiles in the cuisine.

There is more vitamin C in chiles than in oranges, and they are also addictive. The heat from the chile forces the body to release endorphins to deal with it, thus making you feel good. The more chiles you eat, the more your tolerance for the heat they provide increases, and so your body needs a hotter dose.

Abundant variety

There are many varieties of chile used across Asia—fresh and dried, large and small, red and green. All these chiles have unique tastes, so it is important to try to match the right ones to the dishes that you are going to make. The heat in a chile comes from the seeds and the central core of white pith. The smaller the chile, the hotter it is—bird's-eye chiles are

Green chile

Dried red chile

Fresh red chiles

Sambal oelek

an example of this. Large finger-length red (ripe) and green (unripe) chiles are usually moderately hot. Another important factor is that the hotter the climate where the chiles are grown, the riper and therefore the hotter the chiles will be.

In India, chiles are mostly used fresh in their green unripe state, but they are still fiery hot. If you make a green masala paste or a curry from South India using fresh green chiles, it is likely to be very spicy. Most of the ripe red chiles that are grown are dried, with much of them being ground into chile powder.

As you head further south throughout tropical Asia, the temperature increases—as does the spiciness of the food. This is true in India, Sri Lanka, Thailand, Malaysia, and Vietnam, to name but a few. You eat hot food to make you sweat, which in turn cools you down. Also, there is a bounty of sweet fruit and nuts such as coconut, papaya, mango, and watermelon in the tropics, and these are used to temper other ingredients that are too hot. Sugar lessens the acidity that is found in chiles.

Different approaches
In Thailand, the main chiles (*prik*) that are used are the finger-length varieties and also the tiny but fiery hot bird's-eye chile, which can be red, orange, yellow, or green. A Thai condiment present on every communal table is *nam pla*, a simple concoction of sliced small chiles that is known as *prik khii nuu* (which translates alarmingly as "mouse-dropping chiles"), floating in *nam pla* (Thai fish sauce). To make a dipping sauce for seafood, minced garlic, lime juice, and a little sugar are added—this is called *nam jim*. Similar condiments are used in Vietnam, Malaysia, and Indonesia.

Chiles can be pickled or preserved, or dry-roasted to impart a distinct smoky taste. Unripe green chiles have a sharp heat and a slightly acidic taste. To lessen the heat of dried chiles, but without reducing flavor, cut them open and remove the seeds, then soak the dried skins in boiling water for about 20 minutes before using. Always wash your hands well after handling chiles, before touching eyes, lips, and other sensitive areas. Being scrupulous about washing your hands will ensure that you don't unintentionally suffer the sting of chile.

"The heat in a chile comes from the seeds and the central core of white pith. The smaller the chile, the hotter it is. Large finger-length red (ripe) and green (unripe) chiles are usually moderately hot."

Sambals

Throughout Malaysia, Indonesia, and Singapore, the sambal rules the table. This fiery chile paste is served as a condiment and can be eaten on the side or spread on particular ingredients (see pp88–9). There are as many sambals, and as many techniques for making them, as there are cooks who use them. Some sambals call for fresh red chiles, while others use dried. A couple use green chiles (see pp44–5). Some are raw; others are fried. At the simplest end of the scale is *sambal oelek*, a combination of chiles, salt, and vinegar. It can be bought in jars and is a good base to start with. Shallots, garlic, galangal, and balacan (shrimp paste) can be added, as well as tamarind pulp and spices. *Sambal ikan bilis* is made with dried anchovies, while *sambal balacan* is a blend of chiles and shrimp paste.

Ban khoai | Happy crêpes

The combination of textures of crispy, soft, and chewy found in this recipe, as well as the grouping of flavors, is typical of Vietnamese cuisine. When making happy crêpes, have a couple of skillets going at the same time, so that you can produce a continuous flow of these fantastic crêpes. They gained their name from the great noise they make when they are cooking.

Serves 4

1 cup rice flour

½ cup cornstarch

¼ cup all-purpose flour

3 scallions (green onions), white and green parts sliced separately

8oz (225g) ground pork

2 tablespoons fish sauce such as nuoc nam

2 garlic cloves, finely chopped

8oz (225g) raw shrimp, peeled, deveined, and coarsely chopped

vegetable oil for cooking

8oz (225g) bean sprouts, trimmed and rinsed

1 small onion, finely sliced

10 large button mushrooms, finely sliced

3 eggs, beaten

freshly ground black pepper

1 Combine the rice flour, cornstarch, and all-purpose flour with the scallion whites and 2 cups water to make a smooth batter the consistency of heavy cream. Combine the pork with half the fish sauce, half the chopped garlic, and half the scallion greens. Season with black pepper.

2 Mix the shrimp with the remaining fish sauce, garlic, and scallion greens. Again, season with black pepper. Arrange in bowls with all the other ingredients near the stove.

3 Heat a small skillet or omelet pan over a medium-high heat. Add a tablespoon of oil. Into the hot pan, put a tablespoon of chopped pork and two or three pieces of prawn; cook for 2 minutes.

4 Reduce the heat to medium, and add 3 tablespoons batter. Add a tablespoon of the bean sprouts and a few slices of onion and mushroom. Cover with a lid, and cook for 2 minutes. Remove the lid, and add 3 tablespoons beaten egg. Cover once again, and cook for a further 2 minutes.

5 Fold the omelet in half, and carry on cooking until the underside is crisp and golden, then turn over and cook on the other side until golden, too, allowing about 2 minutes for each side. Keep the process going, so that you are serving a stream of crêpes, rather than one batch at the end. Serve each happy crêpe immediately, accompanied by *nuoc dau phung*, a light peanut sauce (see p153).

Partner with
Sesame chicken salad with white pepper (pp118–19)
Vietnamese peanut dipping sauce (p153)

Taruang balado | Sumatran eggplant sambal

There are many variations of sambals, the fiery hot chile pastes used in Indonesian and Malaysian cuisine. Some use dried chiles, while others use fresh ones. Some sambals, such as this one, are completely vegetarian, while others use shrimp paste, fish sauce, or dried fish. So many islands and different cultures make up Indonesia that it is not surprising that there is such a melting pot of food styles and ancient culinary influences. Make a larger batch of the sambal, and keep it in the refrigerator to use in stir-fries, noodles, and seafood dishes.

1 To make the sambal paste, halve the tomatoes and remove the seeds. Put a tomato half in the palm of your hand, with the flesh side outermost. Using a box grater, grate the tomato flesh into a bowl, leaving the leftover skin in your hand. Continue until you have grated all the tomato halves, and discard the skin.

2 Using a mortar and pestle, crush the chile with the garlic and salt to make a paste. Add the shallot, and continue to pound to make a smooth purée. Heat the 2 tablespoons oil in a heavy pan over a medium-high heat. Add the chile paste; fry for 4–5 minutes until fragrant. Add the grated tomato pulp, and cook for 2–3 minutes until softened and combined. Season with salt and black pepper, and add the lime juice and 2 tablespoons water. Set aside.

3 Cut the eggplants in half lengthways. Heat the 3 tablespoons oil in a heavy pan over a medium-high heat. Fry the eggplants in batches for about 3 minutes on each side until tender and golden brown. Season with salt and black pepper.

4 Spread the sambal paste on the cut side of the eggplants, and transfer to a serving dish. Serve with lime wedges as part of a larger selection of dishes.

Serves 4

1½ lbs (750g) Japanese eggplants

3 tablespoons vegetable oil

salt and freshly ground black pepper

lime wedges, to serve

For the sambal paste

2 large tomatoes

5 fresh red chiles, seeded and finely chopped

2 garlic cloves, finely chopped

1 teaspoon salt

5 shallots, finely chopped

2 tablespoons vegetable oil

juice of 1 lime

Partner with
Pork balls with garlic and pepper (pp38–9)
Crisp peanut wafers (p65)
Malay beef rendang (pp148–9)

Pe chan gyaw | Burmese spiced split pea fritters

The split peas, cumin seeds, and coriander seeds in these Burmese fritters highlight the recipe's original Indian roots. Yet, despite the influence of Burma's neighbors India, China, and Thailand, Burmese cuisine remains unique and quite distinctive. Serve these fritters with drinks or at the start of a meal.

Serves 6

½ cup (100g) dried yellow split peas, picked and rinsed

1 tablespoon coriander seeds

1 tablespoon cumin seeds

2 garlic cloves

½ teaspoon crushed dried red chile flakes

1 tablespoon vegetable oil plus 1 cup for deep-frying

4 shallots, finely chopped

5 tablespoons rice flour

salt and freshly ground black pepper

1 Soak the dried split peas in cold water to cover overnight. Drain off the soaking liquid, and rinse the split peas under fresh cold water until the water runs clear.

2 Using a mortar and pestle, crush the coriander and cumin seeds until fine. Add the garlic and chile flakes, and continue to pound to make a paste. Heat the 1 tablespoon oil in a small saucepan over a medium-high heat, and add the spice and garlic paste. Fry for 2 minutes until fragrant. Reduce the heat to low, add the shallot, and continue to fry until the shallot is soft and just starting to caramelize. Remove from the heat.

3 Mix the flour and 2 cups water in a bowl to make a batter. Add the soaked split peas and the shallot mixture, and season with salt and black pepper. Heat the extra vegetable oil for deep-frying in a wok or high-sided heavy pan. When the oil is hot, test a little piece of the batter—it should sizzle immediately. Gently drop a heaping tablespoonful of batter in the hot oil. Fry for about 2 minutes until golden brown. Remove from the oil and, when cooled slightly, taste the fritter and adjust the seasoning for salt and pepper.

4 When the seasoning is right, carefully spoon tablespoons of the batter into the hot oil, and deep-fry for 2–3 minutes until crisp and golden. Deep-fry only a few fritters at a time, and remove from the oil with a slotted spoon before draining on paper towels. Keep frying in batches until all the batter has been used. Serve hot.

Partner with
Isaan-style grilled chicken (pp40–1)
Sri Lankan smoky eggplant dip (pp150–1)

Hot and steamy

There is something supremely comforting about food that has been slow-cooked, simmered, or steamed, to be brought to the table for everyone to enjoy. It can also be supremely tasty, benefiting from the addition of herbs, spices, and condiments that lift the food from mere comfort eating into something singular to savor. Chinese steamed dumplings, hot spicy soups, a sumptuous pilaf from the culinary treasure trove of what was once the Persian empire—these Asian dishes range from what may be familiar favorites to the more exotic.

Taugeh masak kerang | Fried bean sprouts and clams

The sweetness of clams and mussels, as well as the ease of cooking them, makes them a favorite in any coastal region where their freshness can be assured. This very simple dish consists of only a few ingredients, but the flavors are fantastic. Roll up your sleeves and enjoy—there really is no elegant way of eating this.

Serves 4

2¼lb (1kg) clams, scrubbed and cleaned

1¼in (3cm) piece of fresh ginger

3 celery stalks, white central part of stem only

3 tablespoons vegetable oil

2 fresh red chiles, seeded and finely chopped

3 garlic cloves, inner green shoots removed, thinly sliced

14oz (400g) bean sprouts, rinsed

1 tablespoon soy sauce

juice of 1 lime

1 small bunch of fresh cilantro, leaves picked

salt and freshly ground black pepper

1 Rinse the clams under plenty of cold running water. Remove any dirt or barnacles with a knife. Keep rinsing until the water is completely clear. Discard any clams that do not close when they are tapped on the work surface, as they are dead. Also discard any with an off odor or with broken shells. Cut the ginger into thin slices, then finely shred into thin matchsticks. Cut the celery into 1¾in (4cm) lengths, then cut these into matchsticks as well.

2 Heat a heavy pan large enough to hold the clams over a medium-high heat. Add half the oil, and fry half of the chile, garlic, and ginger for 1–2 minutes until fragrant. Add the clams and a splash of water to steam. Cover with a lid and cook over a high heat, shaking the pan occasionally, for 2 minutes. Remove the lid, and stir the contents from the bottom. Cook for a further 2 minutes until the clams have all opened (discard any that do not). Set a colander lined with a clean piece of cheesecloth or dish towel over a bowl. Strain the clams, trapping any specks of grit or sand in the cloth, and reserve the strained cooking liquor.

3 Heat a wok over a medium-high heat, and add the remaining oil. Fry the remaining chile, garlic, and ginger for 1 minute until fragrant. Add the celery, and stir-fry for a further minute. Next, add the bean sprouts, and stir-fry vigorously for 1 minute. Finally, add the cooked clams, reserved cooking liquor, soy sauce, and lime juice. Season with plenty of black pepper, and stir in the cilantro. Taste the sauce and adjust the seasoning. It should be hot, sweet, salty, and sour. Stir through, divide among four bowls, and serve immediately.

Partner with
Marinated grilled mackerel (pp22–3)
Burmese spiced split pea fritters (pp90–1)

Miso shiru | Miso soup with seven-spice chicken

Miso is a paste made from fermented soya beans and a grain—either barley or rice. It is aged for up to three years to mellow the flavors. There are about six basic types, ranging in texture and color from pale yellow to a deep chocolate brown; each has its own savory taste. If you can, try to use the least commercially processed product that is available, as the taste will be superior. Miso provides a base for a soup to which you can add an array of ingredients—mushrooms, seafood, grilled meat, or tofu.

1 Heat a ridged cast-iron grill pan until very hot. Season the chicken breasts with salt, black pepper, and the shichimi togarashi. Grill the chicken until golden brown and cooked on both sides, allowing about 4 minutes on each side depending on the size.

2 Bring the dashi stock to the boil, add the miso paste, and gently dissolve. Remove from the heat, and add the scallion, ginger, and soy sauce to the stock.

3 Slice the chicken into thin pieces, and divide among four serving bowls. Pour the stock over the chicken, dividing the ginger and scallion evenly. Serve immediately, with extra soy sauce if required. There will be a balance between the sweet chicken and the hot spices and ginger. The stock will be sour from the miso and salty from the bonito flakes and soy sauce. The kombu that was used in the stock, meanwhile, acts as a flavor enhancer, intensifying all the flavors on your taste buds.

Dashi stock Put a 2½ x 1¾in (6 x 4cm) piece of dried kombu (kelp) in a pan, and cover with 4 cups water. Bring to the boil, uncovered. Just before the water starts boiling, remove the kombu and discard. Sprinkle in 1oz (30g) package bonito flakes, and remove the pan from the heat. When the bonito flakes have sunk to the bottom of the pan, strain the liquid and discard the flakes. You now have a basic stock that can be flavored with light soy sauce, rice wine, ginger, or mushrooms. It can be stored in the refrigerator until needed.

Serves 4

2 large boneless chicken breasts, about 1lb (450g)

½ teaspoon shichimi togarashi (Japanese seven-spice) (available from Japanese or Asian markets)

1 quart (4 cups) dashi stock (see below)

3 tablespoons (4oz) miso paste (available from Japanese markets and health food shops)

4 scallions (green onions), finely chopped

1¾in (4cm) piece of fresh ginger, cut into matchsticks

2 tablespoons light soy sauce plus extra if needed

salt and freshly ground black pepper

Partner with
Steamed barbecue pork buns (p101)
Sashimi of sea bass with hot dressing (p143)

Har gau | Steamed shrimp wontons

What I love about eating dim sum is the huge selection of unique morsels that are brought to your table in a seeming never-ending flow. Here wonton pastry wrappers are used; these are made from a soft egg pastry. Water chestnuts are available fresh, frozen, and canned. Canned ones are fine for this dish, but rinse well before using.

Serves 6

6 water chestnuts, peeled

3 scallions (green onions), finely chopped

1 small bunch of fresh chives, finely chopped

¼ teaspoon red chile flakes

2 teaspoons sesame oil

2 tablespoons vegetable oil

1 tablespoon light soy sauce

1 lb (450g) cooked shrimp, peeled, deveined, and coarsely chopped

½ teaspoon salt

1 package round wonton wrappers

egg wash (1 egg yolk mixed with 2 tablespoons water) for sealing pastry

freshly ground black pepper

1 recipe Sesame and Ginger Vinaigrette (see right), to serve

1 Rinse the chestnuts under cold running water, then finely chop. Mix together in a bowl with the scallions and chives. Season well with black pepper, and add the chile flakes, sesame oil, vegetable oil, soy sauce, shrimp, and salt. Stir to mix well, and let stand in the refrigerator for 20 minutes.

2 Lay out only six or seven wonton wrappers at a time—otherwise the pastry will dry out. Place a teaspoonful of filling on one side of a wrapper. Brush the edges with egg wash. Bring one side over the filling, and press the edges together with your finger to seal, making sure that no air bubbles are present.

3 Place the wontons on parchment paper and transfer, paper and all, to a bamboo steamer over boiling water. Steam for 10 minutes. Carefully lift the wontons off the paper and serve immediately, accompanied by the sesame and ginger vinaigrette.

Sesame and ginger vinaigrette Serve this dressing with everything from wontons and dim sum dumplings to rare grilled tuna or seared cubes of beef. Mix together the grated zest and juice of 1 orange, ½ tablespoon grated fresh ginger, ½ teaspoon dried red chile flakes, and ½ teaspoon sugar in a glass jar with a lid. Add the juice of 1 lime, 1 tablespoon rice wine vinegar, 1 tablespoon light soy sauce, 3 tablespoons sesame oil, and 2 tablespoons light vegetable oil. Season with salt and black pepper. Shake well, then check the seasoning. Make sure that all the flavors are blended and that no one in particular overpowers the balance. The dressing keeps in the refrigerator for at least a week.

Partner with
Chinese barbecue spare ribs (pp24–5)
Scallion and chive flower rolls (p110–11)

Chuan wei hun tun | Sichuan chicken dumplings

Sichuan cooking is famed for its spiciness. Among the ingredients used to achieve this are Sichuan peppercorns. Although called pepper, they are actually dried berries from the flowering shrub called *fagara*. Sichuan pepper should be a mid red-brown and has a sharp lemony taste which causes a slight numbing to the tongue.

Makes 30 dumplings

8oz (225g) fresh spinach, stemmed

½ teaspoon ground Sichuan peppercorns (see note)

½ teaspoon ground white pepper

2 tablespoons vegetable oil

1½ cups bean sprouts, rinsed

1 teaspoon salt

10oz (300g) ground chicken

1 egg, lightly beaten

1¾in (4cm) piece of fresh ginger, finely chopped

2 tablespoons Shaoxing rice wine

30 square wonton wrappers

For the hot sauce

1 garlic clove

½ teaspoon sugar

4 tablespoons light soy sauce

½ teaspoon ground cinnamon

2 tablespoons chile oil

1 tablespoon rice vinegar

3 scallions, finely sliced

Partner with
Sichuan peppered beef (pp170–1)
Fried eggplant with toasted sesame seeds (p178)

1 To make the hot sauce, use a mortar and pestle to crush the garlic and sugar to a smooth paste. Mix with the remaining ingredients. Set aside. Rinse the spinach in cold water two or three times. Leave to drain in a colander, shaking to remove any excess water. Mix together the Sichuan and ground white pepper in a bowl.

2 Heat the oil in a wok over a medium-high heat. Stir-fry the spinach and bean sprouts until wilted. Season with some of the salt and mixed ground peppers. Remove from the heat; let cool. Stir together the chicken with the egg, ginger, rice wine, and remaining salt and mixed ground pepper. Drain the spinach and bean sprouts, turn out onto a board, and coarsely chop. Combine with the chicken mixture. Fry a little mixture to taste; adjust the seasoning if necessary.

3 Lay out six wonton wrappers at a time on a clean work surface. Put a heaping teaspoonful of chicken mixture onto one half of each wrapper. Brush the edges of the wrappers with a little water. Fold over on a diagonal, and press the edges together. Squeeze the excess air out, away from the dumpling filling. The wontons will be triangular, with the round filling on the inside. Wet your finger and thumb, and press two of the triangle points together; hold for a few seconds until they stick. You will now have a shape that is like a tortellini. Repeat until all the wonton wrappers are used.

4 Bring a large pan of water to the boil. Add the dumplings and simmer for 2–3 minutes. Drain with a slotted spoon, put into serving bowls, and spoon over the sauce. Serve at once.

Note Before grinding, roast the Sichuan peppercorns in a dry frying pan over a medium heat for 2–3 minutes until fragrant.

Char siu bao | Steamed barbecue pork buns

A Chinese staple, these buns are completely addictive. The hot, pillow-like dough is broken open to reveal sweet pork drenched in rich sauce. These steamed gems are frequently served as part of a larger selection of dim sum. They can be prepared in advance, then steamed as needed.

1 To make the dough, put the sugar and water into a mixing bowl. Stir until the sugar has dissolved. Add the yeast, and leave for 10 minutes until it is frothy. Add the oil and baking powder, and sift in the flour. Stir the mixture with your hands, until it comes together as a smooth, slightly wet dough. Cover the bowl with a damp cloth, and allow the dough to rise for 40–60 minutes until it has doubled in size.

2 To make the pork filling, heat the two oils in a wok, and add the garlic, ginger, chile, and mushroom. Stir-fry for 2–3 minutes until fragrant. Add the pork and scallions, stir through, then add the vinegar, sugar, hoisin, and soy sauce. Reduce the heat, and stir-fry for 2–3 minutes until the liquid has almost evaporated. Taste the mixture—it should be sweet from the meat and rich sauce, sour from the vinegar, hot from the chile and ginger, and salty from the sesame oil and light soy sauce. Adjust the seasonings, perhaps with a little lemon juice or black pepper. Remove from the heat and leave to cool.

3 Punch down the dough with your fist, and scrape out it of the bowl onto a floured work surface. (The dough can be used immediately or covered with plastic wrap and refrigerated. Use within 12 hours—otherwise the yeast will start to ferment.) When ready, divide the dough into 12 balls. With a rolling pin, shape each dough ball into a 3in (8cm) round. Place a tablespoon of the pork mixture in the center of each disc. Bring the edges up around the filling, and pinch together to seal tightly.

4 Line a bamboo steamer with a piece of parchment paper. Place the buns on the paper, allowing space for them to rise. Steam for 10–12 minutes, or until the tops of the buns have opened slightly. Serve immediately while they are still piping hot.

Serves 6

½ tablespoon vegetable oil

1 teaspoon sesame oil

2 garlic cloves, finely chopped

1¼in (3cm) piece of fresh ginger, finely chopped

1 fresh red chile, seeded and finely chopped

6 fresh oyster or shiitake mushrooms, diced

14oz (400g) Chinese barbecue pork, thinly sliced (see p48, or available from Chinese grocers)

3 scallions (green onions), finely chopped

1 tablespoon rice vinegar

1 teaspoon palm sugar or brown sugar

2 tablespoons hoisin sauce

1 tablespoon light soy sauce

a little freshly squeezed lemon juice (optional)

freshly ground black pepper

For the yeast bun dough

1 tablespoon superfine sugar

1 cup lukewarm water

1½ teaspoons dried yeast

1 tablespoon vegetable oil

1½ teaspoons baking powder

3⅓ cups all-purpose flour

Keynotes | **Rice and noodles**

Rice is such an important crop the world over, with half the population of the planet consuming it two or three times a day. China is credited with the earliest cultivation of this important plant, dating back to Neolithic times. Thousands of varieties are grown throughout Asia, cooked in different ways and eaten during various seasons. Connossieurs claim that they can tell the difference in taste between rice harvested at different times, or the type of rice being cooked just by its smell. Despite the huge number of different varieties, two main types predominate: long-grain and short-grain rice.

Long-grain and short-grain rice

Long-grain rice is the most commonly used rice in India, China, Thailand, Vietnam, and throughout Southeast Asia. It cooks up into easily separated fluffy grains. Basmati rice is the most widely planted variety in India. With its silky texture and superior aroma, it is used for aromatic rice pilafs, birianis, and masala rice. Basmati is also the most exported of the Indian varieties of rice. In China, Vietnam, Thailand, and other parts of Southeast Asia, refreshingly fragrant jasmine long-grain rice is the most popular.

Short-grain rice is favored in Japan and Korea because it has a shorter growing season and can be eaten with chopsticks. Slightly stickier than long-grain, short-grain rice is eaten with savory dishes in Japan and Korea; in Southern China and Vietnam, it is commonly used for rice porridge.

Soba noodles

Black glutinous rice

Rice vermicelli

Basmati rice

Flat rice noodles

Rice paper wrappers

In Vietnam, rice paper wrappers are called *banh trang* and used for Vietnamese spring and summer rolls, or wrapping meat or seafood. They can be fried or used fresh. To make the wrappers, a batter is made from rice flour, water, and salt. A pancake of this batter is then steamed, before being dried on bamboo mats in the sun. I went to a Vietnamese

> "Noodles are intrinsic to life in many parts of Asia such as China, Japan, and Korea. They originated in China more than 2,000 years ago, and have been made commercially for centuries."

village that made them; the entire place was viewed through these translucent discs with their distinctive basketweave pattern—it was quite surreal. Rice paper wrappers are sold dried in packets.

Rice noodles

Noodles are intrinsic to life in many parts of Asia such as China, Japan, and Korea. They originated in China more than 2,000 years ago, and have been made commercially for centuries. Fresh and dried noodles are available in all shapes and sizes.

Fresh noodles are called *fen* in China. There are four main sizes that refer to the width: flat, round, fine, and very fine. They are eaten in a number of ways—stir-fried, in soups, or with a sauce.

Dried rice noodles are made much in the same way as rice paper, and are called "rice sticks." The thinnest variety is rice vermicelli, used in salads and cold dishes, or in stir-fries and soups. Other rice sticks are about ¼ in (5mm) wide like a ribbon and about the length of a chopstick. These are soaked in warm water before adding to soups or stir-fries.

Also made from rice flour, dried thick laksa noodles resemble spaghetti. There may be many variations of laksa, but the type of noodles used is consistent throughout Malaysia and Singapore.

Other noodles

Fresh egg noodles, known as *mein* or Hokkien noodles, are made with wheat. Dried wheat noodles are also made, and either packed in lengths or rolled like a tight bird's nest. Cellophane noodles (*dong fen*) are made from mung bean flour. Transparent when cooked, they are often used in soups and salads. In Japan, egg noodles are called *ramen*, while soba noodles are made from buckwheat and mostly eaten in the north. They are usually pale brown, but some are green and flavored with green tea. Round or flat udon noodles are made from wheat flour and are white in color; they are readily available.

Glutinous rice

Glutinous rice is a type of short-grain rice that is often referred to as "sticky rice." The rice is first soaked for between 5 and 8 hours, then drained and steamed on a clean cloth or piece of muslin in a bamboo steamer for 30–40 minutes. The rice grains become thick, firm, and translucent. Glutinous rice is never really eaten on its own, but often mixed with savoury ingredients such as pork or mushrooms, or made into rice cakes that are wrapped in banana leaves. In Thai cooking, after the rice is steamed, it is mixed with thick coconut cream, sugar, and a pinch of salt, and served with ripe mango. When made with fresh coconut, this simple dish is really amazing.

Zarda pilau | Lamb pilaf with saffron and nuts

Pilaf is a spectacular way of cooking rice. Some pilafs are plain, while others are lavish and designed for special occasions and festivals. Spices used also vary enormously, depending on from where in the vast Persian empire the pilaf originated. Char masala is a blend of four spices in equal quantities: cinnamon, cloves, cumin, and black cardamom seeds. Grind the spices using a mortar and pestle or a spice grinder. Grind only a small amount at a time, and store in an airtight container.

Serves 4

1¾lb (800g) leg of lamb, trimmed
  and boned

2½ cups basmati rice

3 tablespoons vegetable oil

2 onions, finely chopped

2 teaspoons char masala

2 bay leaves

2 tablespoons sugar

½ cup sliced almonds

½ cup skinned pistachio nuts

1 teaspoon saffron threads

salt and freshly ground
  black pepper

1 Dice the lamb into ¾in (2cm) cubes. Rinse the rice in several changes of cold water until the water runs clear, then leave to soak in fresh water for 30 minutes.

2 Meanwhile, heat the vegetable oil in a Dutch oven or similar casserole over a medium-high heat. Add the onion, and sauté for 5–6 minutes until soft and starting to turn golden brown. Add the diced lamb and brown on all sides. Sprinkle in the char masala and bay leaves, and cover with 1 cup water. Season with salt and black pepper. Bring to the boil, then reduce to a simmer and cook for 30–40 minutes until the meat is tender. When the meat is ready, remove with the onion from the pan.

3 Put the sugar and ½ cup water into a separate pan. Simmer for about 5 minutes until the sugar has dissolved and the liquid is syrupy. Stir in the almonds, pistachio nuts, and saffron.

4 Preheat the oven to 300°F (150°C). Bring 1½ quarts water to the boil in a clean pan. Drain the soaked rice, parboil for 3 minutes, then drain again in a large sieve. Mix a quarter of the rice into the syrup and nuts. Add the remaining rice to the meat juices in the Dutch oven or casserole. Top one half of the rice in the casserole with the cooked lamb and the other half with the rice and nut mixture. Cover with a tight-fitting lid, and transfer to the oven. Slow-cook at this low temperature for 45 minutes. Serve the lamb pilaf on a large platter, garnished with the nut-and-saffron-studded rice.

Partner with
Spiced stuffed eggplant
(p165)
Afghan new year compote
(p191)

Mandu | Steamed green vegetable rolls

A delicious Korean version of the Chinese *char siu bao*, or steamed barbecue pork buns (see p101), these soft, pillowy rolls are filled with a tempting mixture of cabbage and oyster mushrooms. They are eaten as a snack or at the start of a larger meal consisting of many courses.

1 Heat the vegetable oil in a heavy pan over a medium-high heat. Add the garlic, ginger, dried chile, and torn oyster mushrooms. Stir-fry for 4-5 minutes until the mushrooms are golden and the mixture is fragrant. Add the onion, and reduce the heat to medium. Sweat for 4–5 minutes until the onion is soft.

2 Add the cabbage, bok choy, and soy sauce. Season with salt and black pepper. Cover the pan with a lid, and sweat the cabbage over a low heat until soft, but still with a slight bite. Add the lemon juice and sesame oil. Remove from the heat, and turn out the contents of the pan onto a cutting board. Coarsely chop. Allow to cool, then add the scallion.

3 Divide the prepared dough into 12 balls. On a floured work surface, roll each ball into a 3in (8cm) round. Place a tablespoon of the cooked cabbage mixture in the center of each disc. Bring the edges of the dough up around the filling; pinch them together to seal.

4 Line a bamboo steamer with a piece of parchment paper. Place the buns on the paper, allowing space for them to rise. Steam for 10–12 minutes, or until the tops of the buns have opened. Serve immediately while they are still piping hot.

Serves 6

½ tablespoon vegetable oil

2 garlic cloves, finely chopped

1¼in (3cm) piece of fresh ginger, finely chopped

1 small dried red chile, crushed

10 fresh oyster mushrooms, torn into equal pieces

2 onions, finely chopped

½ Chinese cabbage, finely sliced

2 heads bok choy, finely sliced

1 tablespoon light soy sauce

juice of 1 lemon

1 teaspoon sesame oil

3 scallions (green onions), finely chopped

salt and freshly ground black pepper

1 recipe yeast bun dough (see p101)

Partner with
Fresh lettuce cups with chicken (pp124–5)
Chilled soba noodles with seared salmon (pp130–1)

Jiaozi | Mushroom pot-stickers

You can alter the filling in these Chinese dumplings to suit your taste, making them vegetarian, or perhaps using pork, beef, duck, or another combination. They are also very popular in Japan, where they are known as *gyoza*. The dumplings are first fried, before liquid is added to the pan, then finished off by steaming.

1 Soak the dried mushrooms in about ½ cup boiling water to cover for 15 minutes. Heat some of the oil in a heavy pan over a high heat. Sauté a quarter of the field and oyster mushrooms for 4 minutes until well colored, then remove to a bowl. Repeat with the rest of the fresh mushrooms, cooking in batches. Set aside.

2 Drain the shiitakes and coarsely chop, reserving the liquid. Heat a little more oil in the same pan over a medium-high heat; sauté half the garlic and ginger for 1 minute. Add the shiitakes and fry for 3 minutes until browned. Strain the mushroom liquid through a sieve into the pan; cook for 3–4 minutes until absorbed. Add the reserved mushrooms. Season with the 1 teaspoon salt and some black pepper. Remove from the hea, and transfer to a chopping board.

3 Return the pan to a medium heat. Sauté the remaining garlic and ginger in a little oil for 2 minutes until fragrant. Add the shallot, and sweat until soft. Chop the mushrooms into equal sizes. Return to the pan. Add the soy sauce, sesame oil, brown sugar, and black pepper. Cook for 3–4 minutes to combine the flavors. Let cool.

4 Lay out six wonton wrappers at a time. Place 2 teaspoons filling on one half of each one. Brush the edges with a little water. Fold over to make a half-moon. Squeeze the edges tightly together using your thumb and forefinger, then press the base of each dumpling on the work surface so that they will sit upright while cooking. Heat a little oil in a large frying pan over a medium heat. Gently fry the dumplings, bottom-side down, for about 2 minutes until golden brown. Add the rice wine, cover with a lid, and reduce the heat. Steam for 3 minutes until all the liquid is absorbed. Carefully remove the dumplings, and serve with the black vinegar dipping sauce.

Serves 4–6

12 dried shiitake mushrooms

about 4 tablespoons vegetable oil for cooking

8oz (225g) field mushrooms, cut into ¼in (3mm) slices

8oz (225g) oyster mushrooms, torn

3 garlic cloves, finely chopped

2in (5cm) piece of fresh ginger, finely chopped

1 teaspoon salt

3 shallots, finely chopped

1 tablespoon light soy sauce

1 tablespoon sesame oil

1 teaspoon brown sugar

24 wonton wrappers

½ cup Shaoxing rice wine

freshly ground black pepper

1 recipe Black Vinegar Dipping Sauce (p122), to serve

Hua jian | Scallion and chive flower rolls

Numerous variations of these Chinese steamed rolls and buns are frequently eaten as snacks on the street or as part of larger selection of dim sum. These flower rolls are easy to make; however, like much of Asian food, when fresh and made well, they are irresistibly moreish, with a great combination of flavors. Serve them hot.

Makes 6 rolls

1 tablespoon vegetable oil

2 garlic cloves, finely chopped

1 fresh red chile, seeded and finely chopped

2 onions, finely chopped

1 tablespoon light soy sauce

1 tablespoon rice vinegar

8 scallions (green onions), finely chopped

1 bunch of fresh chives, cut into ½in (1cm) lengths

2 tablespoons sesame oil

1 recipe yeast bun dough (see p101)

salt and freshly ground black pepper

Partner with
Stir-fried greens with garlic (p18–19)
Roast pork with fresh mint and peanuts (pp158–9)

1 Heat the vegetable oil in a wok over a medium-high heat, and add the garlic and chile. Cook for 1 minute until fragrant. Add the onion, and stir-fry for 3–4 minutes until soft. Add the light soy sauce and rice vinegar, and cook for a minute or two until all the liquid has been absorbed. Add the scallion and chives. Season with salt and lots of black pepper. Stir-fry for 1 minute until the chives have wilted. Remove from the heat, and leave to cool.

2 Cut the dough in half. Roll out each half on a floured surface to form a 12in x 4in (30cm x 10cm) rectangle. Brush one half of the dough liberally with half of the sesame oil. Spread half the onion and chive mixture over the dough. Lay the other half of dough on top of the onion mixture. Brush again with the sesame oil, then spread out the remaining onion and chive mixture on top of this.

3 Starting with one of the long sides, roll up the dough like a roulade. Pinch the two ends together to keep the sesame oil from seeping out. Lightly flatten the roll with the heel of your hand, then cut the roll into 1¾in (4cm) pieces. Press down into the middle of each piece of dough with a chopstick, parallel to the two cut ends. Pick up each piece of dough by its rounded ends, and pull until they meet underneath the roll. Pinch the ends together. This will cause the ends to "flower" when they are steamed.

4 Line a bamboo steamer with a piece of parchment paper. Place the buns on the paper, allowing space for them to rise. Steam for 10–12 minutes until the tops of the buns have "flowered." Serve immediately while they are still piping hot.

Laksa lemak | Singapore coconut laksa

There are two main styles of laksa in Singapore, *Penang laksa* and *laksa lemak*, with countless variations on those. This soup is a *laksa lemak*, which is spicy with a rich coconut cream sauce. There version here is made with fish and seafood, but chicken or tofu and vegetables are used frequently.

Serves 6

14oz (400g) unpeeled raw shrimp

4 garlic cloves, any green inner shoots removed, chopped

2 teaspoons freshly ground coriander seeds

1 teaspoon ground turmeric

4 fresh red chiles, seeded and finely chopped

8 shallots, finely chopped

1 teaspoon shrimp paste (balacan)

2 tablespoons macadamia nuts

1lb (450g) rice vermicelli

1 small cucumber

2 lemongrass stalks

2 tablespoons vegetable oil

1 teaspoon salt

1 teaspoon sugar

10fl oz (300ml) coconut cream

8oz (225g) firm-fleshed fish such as snapper or sea bass, cleaned, boned, and cut into ¾in (2cm) cubes

juice of 2 limes

handful of fresh cilantro leaves

8oz (225g) bean sprouts, rinsed

handful of fresh mint leaves

freshly ground black pepper

lime wedges, to serve

1 Bring 2 cups water to the boil. Add the whole shrimp, and cook for 2 minutes until the shrimp turns pink. Remove the shrimp with tongs, and reserve the liquid. When cool enough to handle, peel the shrimp, slit open the backs with a knife, and devein. Set aside.

2 Using a mortar and pestle, grind the garlic, coriander seeds, and turmeric to make a paste. Add the chile and shallot, then the shrimp paste and macadamia nuts, grinding all the while. Add a little water and keep grinding until you have a smooth paste. Set aside.

3 Soak the rice vermicelli in boiling water for 2 minutes until soft; drain. Cut the cucumber into 1¾in (4cm) lengths, then cut the flesh into slices; discard the central core of seeds. Restack the slices and cut the cucumber into matchsticks. Remove the outer leaves of the lemongrass stems, then bruise the stems with back of a knife.

4 Heat the oil in a heavy pan over a medium heat, and add the reserved spice paste. Stir-fry for about 5 minutes until fragrant. Add the reserved shrimp cooking liquor, lemongrass, salt, and sugar, and bring to the boil. When the water has boiled, add the coconut cream. Simmer for 8–10 minutes until the liquid starts to thicken.

5 To serve, divide the noodles among six deep bowls. Season the fish with black pepper; add to the simmering liquid. Poach for 3–4 minutes until cooked. Add half the lime juice and half the fresh cilantra. Check the seasoning. Thirty seconds before you remove the pan from the heat, mix in the reserved shrimp and the bean sprouts. Divide the fish, shrimp, and bean sprouts among the bowls, and ladle the broth over all. Garnish with the remaining cilantro, mint leaves, cucumber, and lime wedges. Serve hot.

Bakwan kepiting | Nonya pork, shrimp, and crab ball soup

Nonya cuisine is very creative and distinctive; it is a blend of Chinese and Malaysian influences, with Indonesian and Thai overtones. The food is noted for its abundant use of fresh cilantro, yet fewer dried spices than are found in typical Malay cuisine. Coriander, cumin, and fennel seeds are the main choices.

1 Cover the shiitake mushrooms in boiling water and soak for 30 minutes. Drain the mushrooms and finely chop, reserving the mushroom liquid. Slice the asparagus spears on an angle, into 3cm 1¼in (3cm) spears. Set aside.

2 To make the meatballs, combine the chopped mushrooms, pork, shrimp, crab meat, chile, scallion, egg, and cornstarch in a bowl. Season well with salt and black pepper. Take a small piece of mixture and fry it in a small frying pan. Taste the mixture, and adjust the seasoning to suit your taste.

3 To make the soup, heat the vegetable oil in a heavy pan over a medium-high heat. Fry the garlic slivers for 1–2 minutes until golden brown and crisp. Remove the garlic with a slotted spoon, and drain on paper towels. Pour in the chicken stock and bring to the boil, then reduce to a simmer. Add the soy sauce and reserved mushroom liquid to the stock.

4 Meanwhile, shape the pork mixture into balls about 1in (2.5cm) in diameter. Drop the balls into the simmering liquid—they will take 4–5 minutes to cook. When ready, they will float to the surface.

5 Two minutes before serving, add the asparagus spears. Taste the soup and adjust the seasoning with salt, black pepper, and a little lime juice, which will highlight the flavors. Add the bean sprouts a minute before removing the soup from the heat. Ladle the soup into serving bowls, and add the poached pork balls. Garnish with the slivers of fried garlic and lots of fresh cilantro.

Serves 4–6

2 dried shiitake mushrooms

8 fresh asparagus stems

8oz (225g) lean ground pork

5oz (150g) raw shrimp, peeled, deveined, and finely chopped

5oz (150g) crab meat, picked over

2 fresh red chiles, seeded and finely chopped

3 scallions (green onions), finely chopped

1 egg, lightly beaten

½ teaspoon cornstarch

1 tablespoon vegetable oil

3 garlic cloves, any green inner shoots removed, slivered

1 quart (4 cups) chicken stock

2 tablespoons light soy sauce

juice of 1 lime

1½ cups bean sprouts, rinsed

handful of fresh cilantro leaves

salt and freshly ground black pepper

Partner with
Stir-fried bean sprouts with chile bean paste (p21)
Burmese turmeric fishcakes (pp80–1)

Sambal babi | Nonya-style spicy pork

This simple pork dish from Singapore bears all the characteristic well-balanced flavor of Nonya cuisine. Hot, sweet, salty, and sour are all represented. It works particularly well when eaten as part of a larger meal.

Serves 4

1lb (450g) pork

4 dried red chiles

8 shallots, chopped

1 teaspoon shrimp paste (balacan)

2 tablespoons vegetable oil

3 tablespoons tamarind pulp (see p154)

1 teaspoon sugar

1 tablespoon light soy sauce

handful of fresh cilantro leaves

salt and freshly ground black pepper

1 Cut the pork into slices about ½in (1cm) thick, then cut those slices into pieces 5cm (2in) long and ½in (1cm) wide. Soak the dried chiles in 1 cup boiling water to soften. Remove the seeds and discard, and finely chop the flesh.

2 Using a mortar and pestle, pound the chile, shallot, and shrimp paste to a fine paste. Heat the vegetable oil in a wok over a medium heat. Fry the paste gently for 4–5 minutes until fragrant.

3 Add the pork slices, and cook until brown on all sides and coated in the spice paste. Add the tamarind pulp and sugar, and season with salt and black pepper. Finally, add the light soy sauce and enough cold water to almost cover the meat. Simmer, uncovered, stirring the mixture frequently to the meat from sticking to the pan. When the sauce has reduced and thickened, add the cilantro leaves and serve hot.

Partner with
Sardines with green chile sambal (pp46–7)
Nonya bean curd salad (pp136–7)

Fresh and aromatic

Across the many Asian cuisines, the word "fresh" need not apply only to salads, although there is certainly a wealth of these to choose from all across this vast region—and indeed in this chapter. Fresh herbs, crisp vegetables, fresh fruits and nuts, cooling yogurt and sauces are all used to best advantage. But there are also the other "fresh" approaches such as chilled seafood, fresh-tasting chutneys, even using fresh herbs and greens for wrapping food. And all come with that Asian aromatic pull of spices and seasonings.

Sesame chicken salad with white pepper

There are many variations of chicken salad in Southeast Asia and China. This one originates from China's Yunnan province, near the borders of Burma, Vietnam, and Laos. Vibrantly flavored with great textures, it bears similarities to dishes from each of these countries with its use of cilantro and chiles. It can be served as a meal in itself with rice or noodles, or as part of a larger Asian meal where it is one of many dishes.

Serves 4–6

6 celery stalks from the center of the bulb

handful of fresh cilantro, leaves picked (keep the stems)

1¾in (4cm) piece of fresh ginger, finely chopped (reserve the peelings for the stock)

6 white peppercorns

3 whole skinless chicken breast fillets, 1–1¼lbs (450–600g)

2 garlic cloves, any green inner shoot removed, finely chopped

2 fresh green chiles, seeded and finely chopped

4 scallions (green onions), finely chopped

2 tablespoons light soy sauce

2 tablespoons rice wine vinegar

½ teaspoon salt

1 teaspoon sugar

1 teaspoon ground white pepper

2 tablespoons sesame oil

2 tablespoons sesame seeds

Partner with
Steamed green vegetable rolls (p105)
Tamarind fried shrimp (pp154–5)

1 Bring a saucepan of water to the boil, and add 2 of the celery stalks, the cilantro stems, the ginger peelings, and 6 white peppercorns. When the stock is boiling, add the chicken breasts and return the boil. Simmer for 5 minutes, using a slotted spoon to skim off any scum that rises to the surface. Cover the pan with a lid, and remove from the heat. Let stand for 20 minutes—the poached chicken will be perfectly cooked and juicy. After 20 minutes, remove the chicken from the pan and allow to cool. (You can reserve the chicken stock for another use.)

2 Cut the remaining celery into thin slices, then restack and cut into thin matchsticks. Bring a little water to the boil in a small pan, and blanch the celery for 10 seconds, then refresh under cold running water to stop the cooking. Drain and set aside.

3 To make the dressing, mix the garlic, chile, and chopped ginger in a bowl with the scallion, light soy sauce, rice wine vinegar, salt, sugar, and white pepper. Let stand to combine the flavors. Take the poached chicken and pull apart into shreds about ½in (1cm) wide and 1¼in (3cm) long. Mix the shredded chicken with the celery and sesame oil. Add the dressing, and leave to stand for 5 minutes.

4 Meanwhile, in a small frying pan over a medium heat, dry-roast the sesame seeds for 3–4 minutes until they pop and turn golden brown. Tear the cilantro leaves into the chicken salad, then sprinkle over the sesame seeds. Toss together and serve.

Katsuo tataki | Chilled seared tuna with ginger

This is a simple way of transforming fresh tuna to form part of a summer Asian meal. The tuna is seared, then marinated, with both methods imparting their effects on flavor and texture. This method works equally well with fillet beef or venison. The tangy dressing works brilliantly with the sweetness of the fish.

1 Heat a heavy frying pan over a medium-high heat. Take the piece of tuna, and cut it in half across the grain. Cut each piece in half lengthways again, so there are four quarter pieces shaped like logs. Roll the tuna logs in the sesame seeds, and season well with salt, black pepper, and the shichimi togarashi.

2 Tear off 4 pieces of aluminum foil and keep them by the frying pan. Grease the heated frying pan with a little oil, and sear the tuna for 20–30 seconds on one side until the sesame seeds turn golden. Carefully turn the tuna over with tongs, and sear on the other side. Remove the tuna from the pan, and place each piece onto a separate piece of foil. Tightly roll the tuna in the foil, like a cigar. Put the foil parcels in the freezer for 30 minutes. This will stop the cooking and firm up the tuna's texture for easy slicing.

3 Meanwhile, prepare the other ingredients. Finely slice the ginger, then restack on the work surface. Cut thinly into matchsticks. Crush the garlic with a little salt using the back of a chopping knife to form a paste. Mix the garlic paste with the lemon juice, mirin, rice vinegar, and tamari. Transfer the dressing to a shallow dish.

4 Remove the tuna from the freezer, take out of the foil, and place in the dish with the dressing. Add half the ginger and half the scallions. Let marinate for 10 minutes, turning regularly so the dressing is absorbed into the fish. After 10 minutes, remove the tuna and place on a board. Using a knife, cut into thin slices about 1/8in (2–3mm) thick. Each slice will be rare in the center with a seared sesame edge. Arrange on individual plates or a large platter, and spoon on the dressing. Sprinkle the remaining ginger and scallion over the tuna and serve.

Serves 4

1lb (450g) fresh tuna, in one large piece

4 tablespoons sesame seeds

1 teaspoon shichimi togarashi (Japanese seven-spice, (available at Japanese or Asian markets)

a little vegetable oil

1¾in (4cm) piece of fresh ginger

1 garlic clove, any green inner shoot removed, finely chopped

juice of ½ lemon

2 tablespoons mirin

2 tablespoons rice wine vinegar

3 tablespoons tamari (Japanese soy sauce)

4 scallions (green onions), finely chopped

salt and freshly ground black pepper

Partner with
Marinated barbecue beef (pp52–3)
Hot and sour green papaya salad (pp144–5)

Ponzu | Citrus dipping sauce

Ponzu is served with fresh fish and shellfish, whether it is raw, seared, or lightly cooked. The name comes from the time when there were Dutch traders in Japan. *Pon* comes from the Dutch word for citrus, and *zu*, or *su*, the Japanese word for vinegar. All the ingredients for this dressing are available from Asian food stores and health food shops. It needs to be made at least 24 hours in advance, but it keeps for a long time in the refrigerator so you always make a large quantity.

Makes enough for 6–8 servings

3in x 2½in (8cm x 6cm) piece of kombu (Japanese dried kelp)

1 cup lemon juice

1 cup lime juice

½ cup rice wine vinegar

½ cup mirin (Japanese rice wine)

5 tablespoons tamari (Japanese soy sauce)

1½ oz (40g) dried bonito flakes

1 Using tongs, carefully hold the piece of kombu over a gas flame for 10–15 seconds on each side. Put the kombu in a bowl with the lemon and lime juices, vinegar, mirin, tamari, and bonito flakes. Cover and marinate in the refrigerator for 24 hours.

2 Strain the sauce into a serving bowl, and discard the solids. Use as a dipping sauce for sushi, sashimi, tempura, or fried shellfish and seafood.

Black vinegar dipping sauce Chinkiang black vinegar comes from northern China and has a complex smoky flavor; it is aged in a similar fashion to balsamic vinegar. This Chinese dipping sauce goes spectacularly well with the pot-stickers on pp106–7, but can be used whenever a vinegar dipping sauce is called for. To make, put ⅔ cup Chinkiang black vinegar, 1 teaspoon sugar, and a 1¼in (3cm) piece of fresh ginger, grated, in a small pan. Bring to the boil. Simmer for 2 minutes, then remove from the heat and add 2 finely chopped scallions (green onions). Serve as an accompaniment.

Partner with
Shrimp and chive spring rolls (pp72–3)
Sesame tempura (pp78–9)

Kung sang wa | Cured shrimp with shredded lime leaves

A refreshing salad, this works well as a party appetizer. It takes about 10 minutes to put together the ingredients that can be prepared ahead of time and about 4 minutes to cure the shrimp just before serving. It is important that the fibrous and strong-tasting ingredients are shredded to allow all the invigorating flavors to be combined in one mouthful. Use other grilled shellfish such as crayfish, lobster, or crab instead of shrimp if you wish—they provide the same sweetness needed for this dish.

1 Using a hot barbecue or ridged cast-iron grill pan, grill the shrimp whole in their shells for 2 minutes on each side. When cool, peel and devein, then finely shred the meat and set aside.

2 Remove the tough outer layer of the lemongrass, and finely slice the stem. Peel and cut the ginger into thin slices. Restack the slices in piles, and finely shred. Cut the shallots in half through the core; slice as finely as possible so that the slivers are held together at the core. On the back of the kaffir lime leaves there is a raised stem. Using a knife, shave the stem so that the leaves lie flat. Tightly roll the leaves into a cigar shape. Working the knife rhythmically, finely shred the rolled lime leaves into needle-like threads.

3 Mix the lime and orange juices with the fish sauce in a bowl, and stir in the sugar to dissolve. Add the shrimp and the shredded lime leaves for 3 minutes while removing the mint and cilantro leaves from their stems. Roll up the mint leaves and shred them in a similar way to the lime leaves. Tear the cilantro leaves into pieces. Add the chile and scallion to the mixture, then the cilantro and mint. Taste the perfumed mixture. The shrimp and the sugar provide the sweetness; the chile will be hot; the lime juice, lime leaves, and lemongrass are sour; and the fish sauce provides the saltiness. Adjust the seasoning to suit your taste. Serve immediately.

Serves 6

12 large unpeeled raw shrimp

2 lemongrass stalks

1¾in (4cm) piece of fresh ginger

4 shallots

5 tender kaffir lime leaves

2 tablespoons lime juice

2 tablespoons orange juice

2 tablespoons fish sauce such as nam pla

1 teaspoon sugar

4 sprigs of fresh mint

4 sprigs of fresh cilantro

2 medium-hot fresh red chiles, seeded and finely chopped

3 scallions (green onions), finely sliced

Partner with
Seared scallops with fresh chutney (pp16–17)
Grilled beef patties with shallots and cumin (pp26–7)

San choy bau | Fresh lettuce cups with chicken

San choy bau roughly translates as "raw vegetable," the name given to this dish because of the fresh, crisp lettuce leaves that are used as wrappers for these warm parcels. It is a dish filled with contrasting flavors and textures. Instead of chicken, try ground pork or a combination of meats. You could also use squab or duck, if you like.

Serves 6 as a starter

1lb (450g) boneless skinless chicken thighs

3 tablespoons Shaoxing rice wine

3 tablespoons light soy sauce

2 teaspoons sesame oil

8 dried shiitake mushrooms

about 12 fresh water chestnuts, peeled

1 teaspoon sugar

1 garlic clove, any green inner shoot removed, finely chopped

1¾in (4cm) piece of fresh ginger, finely chopped

2 fresh red chiles, seeded and finely chopped

4 scallions (green onions), finely chopped

vegetable oil for cooking

12 crisp butter lettuce leaves

salt and freshly ground black pepper

Partner with
Grilled marinated mackerel (pp22–3)
Sichuan spicy pickled cucumber (p152)

1 Put the chicken in a food processor with 2 tablespoons of the rice wine, 1 tablespoon of the light soy sauce, and 1 teaspoon of the sesame oil. Process until finely chopped. Transfer to a bowl, cover, and refrigerate for 1–2 hours. Put the dried mushrooms in a bowl; cover with boiling water. Let stand for 30 minutes. Drain, saving the soaking liquid and squeezing excess liquid from the mushrooms into the bowl. Discard the stems and chop the caps. Set aside.

2 Blanch the water chestnuts in a pan of boiling water for 1 minute, then refresh in cold water. Roughly chop and set aside. Mix ¼ cup of the reserved mushroom soaking liquid with the remaining 1 tablespoon rice wine, 2 tablespoons light soy sauce, and 1 teaspoon sesame oil. Add the sugar and stir to dissolve. Set aside.

3 Heat a wok until very hot, add 2 tablespoons vegetable oil, and swirl it around to coat the wok. Add the garlic, ginger, chile, and scallion, and stir-fry for 20 seconds. Add the chicken mixture. Stir-fry for 3–4 minutes until the chicken is browned, breaking up the meat so it cooks evenly. Transfer the chicken mixture to a bowl and set aside. Clean the wok and return to the heat, adding a couple of tablespoons of extra oil. Add the mushrooms and water chestnuts, and stir-fry over a high heat for 1 minute.

4 Add the combined mushroom/soy sauce liquid, and bring to the boil for 1–2 minutes. Return the chicken to the wok, and continue stir-frying until the liquid has almost evaporated. Season with salt and black pepper. Put the chicken in a serving bowl surrounded by the lettuce leaves. To eat, spoon some warm chicken onto a lettuce leaf, and fold the lettuce around to make a parcel.

Khayanthee thoke | Grilled eggplant salad

Burmese has a unique cuisine within Asia, taking its influences from its two neighbors India and China, as well as ingredients and styles of cooking from Laos, Thailand, and across Southeast Asia. The many varieties of noodles used in Burma are a result of the Chinese influence, and the use of cumin, coriander seeds, turmeric, beans, and lentils comes from India. There are also numerous fermented fish and seafood products from shrimp pastes to fish sauce found in Burmese cuisine, similar to those used in other parts of Southeast Asia.

Serves 4–6

½ cup skinned raw peanuts

2 large eggplants

1 onion

2 tablespoons vegetable oil

4 garlic cloves, any inner green shoots removed, cut into slivers

1 tablespoon sesame seeds

½ tablespoon tamarind pulp (see p154)

1 tablespoon fish sauce such as nam pla

2 fresh red chiles, seeded and finely chopped

small handful of fresh cilantro leaves, coarsely chopped

popadums, to serve (optional)

1 Spread the peanuts out in a single layer on a baking sheet, and roast in a preheated oven at 400°F (200°C) for 4–5 minutes until golden brown. Set aside. Preheat the broiler. Grill the eggplants under the broiler until the skin is blackened all over and the eggplants are soft. Allow them to cool, then peel off the charred skin and discard. Lightly mash the flesh in a bowl with a fork, then set aside. Finely slice the onion, then soak in cold water for 10 minutes. Drain.

2 Meanwhile, heat the oil in a small saucepan over a medium-high heat and add the garlic slivers. Fry for 1–2 minutes until pale golden and crisp. Make sure that the garlic does not get too dark—otherwise it will become bitter. Remove the garlic to a bowl with a slotted spoon and set aside. Reserve the oil. Using a small heavy frying pan, dry-roast the sesame seeds for 1–2 minutes until they pop and turn golden brown. Remove from the heat.

3 Put the mashed eggplant and drained soaked onion in a bowl. Crush the roasted peanuts with the blade of a knife, and sprinkle over the vegetables with the toasted sesame seeds. Whisk together the tamarind pulp, fish sauce, chopped chile, and reserved garlic oil in a bowl to make a dressing. Pour over the eggplant salad. Serve as a salad, with the cilantro sprinkled over the top. Alternatively, arrange small piles of the salad on broken pieces of popadum, then garnish with the cilantr and serve as a snack or canapé.

Partner with
Sumatran minced duck sate (pp50–1)
Crisp peanut wafers (p65)
Malay beef rendang (pp148–9)

Chilled soba noodles with seared salmon

Japanese soba noodles, made from buckwheat, can be served either hot or chilled. Here they are presented as part of a refreshing salad. Shrimp, chicken, and all kinds of vegetables go well with soba noodles. Although fresh soba noodles are preferable, dried ones work, too. Just follow the package instructions for cooking. Once the noodles are cooked, rinse them in plenty of cold water to wash away the starch.

1 Cut the asparagus into 1¼in (3cm) pieces on an angle, so that the pieces look like pen nibs. To make the dressing, combine the ginger and wasabi paste in a bowl, then add the soy sauce, sesame seeds, vinegar, and dashi stock.

2 Heat a ridged cast-iron grill pan or griddle over a high heat (there is no need to oil the pan). Season the salmon fillets with salt and black pepper. Grill for 2 minutes on each side so that the salmon is rare in the center. The fish will continue to cook when it comes off the grill; by the time it has cooled, it will be medium rare.

3 In the meantime, put the asparagus in a bowl and coat them with a little vegetable oil. Season with salt and black pepper. Toss the asparagus in the bowl so that the seasoning sticks to the asparagus. Grill the asparagus in the cast-iron ridged grill pan until charred on each side, about 4 minutes in total. Do not overcook or it will become soggy—you want it to still have bite. At the same time, roast the sesame seeds in a dry frying pan over a low heat for a few minutes until golden brown, taking care not to scorch.

4 Bring a large pan of salted water to boil. Add the noodles and cook for 4–5 minutes until al dente. Drain and plunge the noodles in cold water to chill quickly. Drain again. Put the noodles in a large bowl, and toss with the dressing. Add the chile and scallion, and mix together. Taste the noodles, and adjust the seasoning in the dressing if necessary. Flake the salmon into the noodles, and add the grilled asparagus. Lightly mix together, then sprinkle the sesame seeds over the top. Serve immediately.

Serves 4

1 bunch of fresh asparagus

2 salmon fillets, about 7oz (200g) each

a little vegetable oil

4 tablespoons sesame seeds

1lb (450g) soba noodles

1 fresh red chile, seeded and finely chopped

4 scallions (green onions), finely sliced

salt and freshly ground black pepper

For the dressing

1¾in (4cm) piece of fresh ginger, finely grated

2 teaspoons wasabi paste

3 tablespoons light soy sauce

2 tablespoons sesame seeds

2 tablespoons rice vinegar

½ cup dashi stock (see p97)

Partner with
Miso soup with seven-spice chicken (pp96–7)
Scallion and chive flower rolls (pp110–11)

Manda uppilittathu | South Indian mango pickle

Unripe green mangoes are used in this fantastic mango pickle, as opposed to the sweeter ripe mangoes found in other versions. This condiment is especially good as an accompaniment to fish and vegetable dishes, with its freshness and balance of flavors and textures. If curry leaves are not available, use fresh cilantro leaves instead.

Serves 6

2 unripe green mangoes

5 shallots, finely sliced

3 large fresh green chiles, seeded and finely chopped

1 teaspoon salt

3 tablespoons vegetable oil

½ tablespoon black mustard seeds

2 level teaspoons chili powder

½ teaspoon ground turmeric

1 level teaspoon asafoetida powder

10 curry leaves (preferably fresh)

squeeze of lemon juice (optional)

1 Peel the mango and cut into ½in (1cm) dice. Mix the mango, shallot, and chile together in a bowl, and sprinkle with the salt. Leave to sit for 30 minutes.

2 Heat the oil in a heavy saucepan over a medium-high heat. Add the mustard seeds, and stir for about 30 seconds until they start to pop. Add the remaining spices, curry leaves, and any liquid that has accumulated in the bowl from the salted mango. Heat vigorously for 2 minutes until the spices are fragrant.

3 Pour the spice mixture over the mango. Stir together, check the seasoning, and adjust the salt to taste. You will have a refreshing balance of hot, sweet, salty, and sour. If the sourness is not coming through, refresh the mango pickle with a squeeze of lemon juice. Allow the mixture to cool, then taste again to adjust the seasoning and correct the balance.

Partner with
Keralan spiced lentil and chickpea dumplings (56–7)
Rice flour pancakes (p81)
Carrot pachadi (pp162–3)

Chamandhi | Fresh coconut chutney

This Southern Indian condiment complements grilled fish or chicken dishes perfectly, and it is just as likely to be enjoyed Sri Lanka or Singapore as in India. Be warned: it won't last long after you make it, as it is so tasty it is likely to be readily devoured by guests and cook alike. If you cannot find fresh coconut, use either unsweetened desiccated or shredded coconut that has been soaked in warm water to soften.

1 Using a mortar and pestle, pound the garlic and ginger to a paste. Add the salt and green chile, and continue to mash until smooth. Add the coconut and 2 tablespoons water, and keep pounding together. (If using desiccated or shredded coconut rather than fresh, use 2 tablespoons of the soaking liquid with the coconut to make a thick paste.)

2 Heat the oil in a frying pan over a medium-high heat. Add the mustard seeds, and fry for 20–30 seconds until they start to crackle and become aromatic. Add the shallot, curry leaves, and chile flakes, and cook for 2–3 minutes until softened. Remove from the heat, and mix together with the coconut paste.

3 Add the cilantro leaves and lime juice, and remove the curry leaves from the chutney, as you want only their flavor. Blend well and taste. The coconut will impart sweetness and the chile heat, while the other seasonings cut the potential richness of the coconut. There should be a good balance of all the flavors. Adjust with more salt or lime juice if necessary.

Serves 6–8

1 garlic clove, any inner green shoot removed, finely chopped

¾in (2cm) piece of fresh ginger

½ teaspoon salt

1 fresh green chile, seeded and finely chopped

8oz (225g) grated fresh coconut

1 tablespoon vegetable oil

1 teaspoon brown mustard seeds

1 sprig of curry leaves (preferably fresh)

3 shallots, finely sliced

½ teaspoon dried red chile flakes

30 fresh cilantro leaves

juice of 1 lime

Partner with
Isaan-style grilled chicken
(pp40–1)
Gujarati eggplant fritters
(pp82–3)

Crisp cabbage salad with peanuts

A deliciously crisp and refreshing salad that stimulates all the senses, this dish is visually appealing, with lots of interesting textures and well-blended flavors that wake up your taste buds and leave your mouth alive. It originates from Laos in the center of Southeast Asia, and you will find similar dishes in Thailand, Vietnam, and Singapore.

Serves 4–6

⅔ cup skinned raw peanuts

1 hard white Chinese cabbage

(1¾in) 4cm piece of fresh ginger

1 tablespoon olive oil

6 shallots, finely sliced

1 garlic clove, any green inner shoot removed, finely chopped

2 fresh red chiles, seeded and finely chopped

1 tablespoon brown sugar

juice of 2 limes

3 tablespoons light soy sauce

1 tablespoon rice vinegar

3 scallions (green onions), finely chopped

handful of fresh mint leaves

handful of freshs cilantro leaves

salt and freshly ground black pepper

Partner with
North Vietnamese fish brochettes (pp46–7)
Tamarind beef with peanuts (pp180–1)

1 Preheat the oven to 400°F (200°C). Put the peanuts in a single layer on a baking sheet, and bake for 4 minutes or until golden brown. Remove from the oven and leave to cool, then coarsely crush the peanuts with the flat side of a knife. Set aside. Remove the tough outside leaves of the cabbage and discard. Cut the cabbage in half, and remove the heart. Finely shred the leaves and put in a large bowl. Finely slice the ginger, then rearrange the slices into stacks on the work surface and finely shred into thin matchsticks. Set aside.

2 Heat a large frying pan over a medium-high heat. Add the olive oil and stir-fry half of the shallot for 2 minutes until starting to caramelize. Push the shallot to one side of the pan, and add the garlic and chile. Stir-fry for 1–2 minutes until fragrant. Add the brown sugar and half of the crushed peanuts. Allow the sugar to melt and coat the peanuts. Mix everything in the pan together, remove from the heat, and transfer to a small bowl.

3 Combine the lime juice, soy sauce, and rice vinegar. Pour over the caramelized shallot and peanut mixture. Season with salt and black pepper. Check the seasoning, and adjust if necessary. It will be hot, sweet, salty, and sour. Add 2 tablespoons water to thin the dressing—this does not dilute the flavors; they are supposed to be quite intense.

4 Just before serving, mix the shredded cabbage with the remaining shallot, scallion, and ginger. Tear the mint and cilantro leaves, and add to the cabbage. Dress the cabbage mixture with the warm peanut dressing and serve immediately, with the remaining peanuts sprinkled over the top.

Taukwa goreng | Nonya bean curd salad

Variations of these crunchy vegetable salads are found in Nonya cooking throughout Singapore and Malaysia, as well as in Indonesia. Use sesame seeds instead of nuts if you prefer. Any combination of vegetables can be used—some blanched, others quickly grilled, while leaving others raw.

1 Cut the cucumber in half lengthways, and remove the seeds with a teaspoon. Finely slice the cucumber flesh. Cut four large slices off the sides of the red pepper, leaving the central core of seeds inside. With a knife, remove the white pith and membrane from the pepper slices; discard. Cut the pepper into thin slices. Top and tail the snow peas. Stack two or three of the snow peas on top of each other, and shred into thin matchsticks. Continue until all the snow peas are shredded. Set aside.

2 To make the dressing, dry-roast the nuts in a heavy pan over a medium heat until golden brown. Shake the pan occasionally, and be careful not to scorch the nuts. Remove from the heat, and allow the nuts to cool. Using a mortar and pestle, mash the ginger, chile, and shallot to a paste. Add the roasted nuts and continue to crush, then add the palm sugar and work until smooth. Add the soy sauce, tamarind pulp, and water. Season with salt and black pepper.

3 Heat enough oil for deep-frying in a large heavy pan over a medium-high heat. Wipe the bean curd dry with paper towels, and deep-fry in the hot oil for 4–5 minutes until golden brown all over. Drain on fresh paper towels, and cut into ¼in (½cm) slices.

4 Bring a pan of salted water to the boil. Blanch the snow peas and bean sprouts in the boiling water for 30 seconds, then quickly refresh under cold running water to stop them cooking. Mix the blanched vegetables with the cucumber and red pepper. Sprinkle on the fried bean curd, scallion, and cilantro leaves. Alternatively, lay out the pieces of bean curd, and top each one with a little salad mixture, scallion, and cilantro. Spoon the roast nut and tamarind dressing over the vegetables, and serve the salad immediately.

Serves 4–6

1 large cucumber

1 red sweet pepper

8oz (225g) snow peas

vegetable oil for deep-frying

8oz (225g) firm bean curd

5oz (150g) bean sprouts, rinsed

2 scallions (green onions), finely chopped

handful of fresh cilantro leaves

For the dressing

4 tablespoons skinned raw peanuts or raw cashew nuts

1¼in (3cm) piece of fresh ginger, finely chopped

2 fresh red chiles, seeded and finely chopped

4 shallots, finely chopped

1 tablespoon palm sugar or brown sugar

1 tablespoon dark soy sauce

3 tablespoons tamarind pulp (see p154)

3 tablespoons warm water

salt and ground black pepper

Partner with
Curried sweet corn fritters (pp70–1)
Sumatran eggplant sambal (pp88–9)

Keynotes | **Coriander, basil, and mint**

Fresh herbs are essential to good food all across the vast region of Asia. Cilantro, mint, Thai basil, chives, watercress, Vietnamese mint, shiso, Asian celery, long-leaf coriander, dill, curry leaves—all are used to provide perfumed freshness in the vibrant patchwork of dishes that make up an Asian meal.

In Vietnam, many dishes are served with what is known as a "table salad." This accompanies soups, salads, spring rolls, and curries; diners tear a selection of fresh leaves into their food. A typical table salad includes cilantro leaves, mint, Thai basil, Vietnamese mint, bean sprouts, and lime wedges. Turkish and Central Asian food also feature accompanying bowls of fresh herbs.

Coriander

Coriander (*Coriandrum sativum*) is said to be the most-consumed herb on the planet, spreading its appeal across South, East, Central, and Western Asia; the Middle East; and much of East Africa and South America. Native to the Middle East, it is documented as being in China around 200 BC.

Fresh coriander, or cilantro, heightens the flavor of other ingredients, while also moderating rich flavors with its fresh citrus taste. It is often sold with its roots intact; used chopped and pounded to form a base in curry pastes, sauces, and dressings, these provide an intense depth of flavor for dishes such as Thai green curry. Coriander seeds are a foundation

Thai basil

Cilantro

ingredient in an Asian spice collection and bear little similarity in taste to the fresh herb. They benefit hugely from dry-roasting and are used in Middle Eastern, Indian, Thai, and Malaysian dishes.

Long-leaf, or saw-leaf, coriander (*Eryngium foetidum*) has a more pronounced taste. It is best when chopped finely or cooked, and is found in Vietnamese and Thai cuisine.

Mint

Coriander seeds

"Fresh coriander heightens the flavor of other ingredients, while also moderating rich flavors with its fresh citrus taste."

Coriander (cilantro) root

Basil

Holy basil (*Ocimum tenuiflorum*) is also called sacred basil or tulsi. An important plant in the Hindu religion, it is also used in ayurvedic medicine. Thai basil (*Ocimum basilicum*) is also known as Asian basil and licorice basil, and it has an intense lemony aniseed aroma. It works well with spices such as cinnamon, star anise, and ginger. The common cultivar "Queen of Siam" has dark green leaves with a purple tinge, and purple stems.

Mint

Mint (*Mentha* spp.) is very versatile and widely used throughout Southeast Asia, in particular Vietnam. This herb originated in Greece and from there spread widely into West and Central Asia, and down into India. There are said to be 30 different varieties. Two of the most widely used are common or garden mint, with its sweet smell, and spearmint, which has a narrow leaf with a serrated edge and a distinctive fresh flavor.

Vietnamese mint

Vietnamese mint (*Polygonum odoratum*), or *rau ram*, has many names, including Vietnamese coriander, Cambodian mint, and hot mint, yet it is not actually a true mint. Its dark green spear-shaped leaves flecked with purple have a strong, pungent, and peppery acidic taste—a few leaves go a long way. It is used in Singaporean and Malaysian soups, as well as Thai salads and Vietnamese summer rolls and table salads.

Asian salad with pea shoots and sprouts

Fresh and vibrant with sprouts and shoots, this salad calls for fresh turmeric, available at Chinese, Thai, and other Asian produce markets. When peeled and thinly sliced, fresh turmeric provides a peppery bite to salads and soups. It is worth trying to get hold of some if you have never used it before. Wear rubber gloves when working with fresh turmeric, or its bright orange color will stain your hands. Mix and match sprouts and shoots based on what's available in the market.

Serves 4–6

1¼in (3cm) piece of fresh turmeric

2 limes

1½ cups pea shoots, rinsed

1½ cups mung bean sprouts, rinsed

1½ cups mustard cress shoots, rinsed

1½ cups alfalfa sprouts, rinsed

30 fresh mint leaves

handful of fresh cilantro leaves

2 handfuls of mixed peppery greens including arugula, watercress, and mizuna

2in (5cm) piece of fresh ginger

For the dressing

3 tablespoons extra virgin olive oil

juice of 1 lemon

½ teaspoon ground turmeric (only if fresh turmeric is not being used in the salad)

1 fresh red chile, seeded and finely chopped

1 teaspoon runny honey

salt and freshly ground black pepper

1 Peel the turmeric and, using a vegetable peeler, shave the turmeric root into slivers. Put in a bowl and cover with fresh water until ready to use.

2 Using a thin knife (it could be serrated), cut the skin and pith off the limes. When all the flesh is exposed, hold the fruit in one hand and cut each segment on the inside of the membrane. Keep the lime segments in a bowl to catch any juices. Peel the ginger and slice finely, then stack together and cut into fine matchsticks.

3 Put the shoots and sprouts in a large bowl. Add the herbs and mixed leaves. Combine all the ingredients for the dressing. If you are using fresh turmeric, drain first, then add to the dressing; if not, simply add the ground turmeric with the other dressing ingredients. (The honey in the dressing softens some of the acidity and the peppery elements of the salad.) Add the ginger, lime segments, and any extra lime juice. Season well with salt and black pepper.

4 Pour the dressing over the sprouts and leaves, and toss gently to a form a vibrant, vitamin-packed combination of textures and flavors that will exercise your taste buds. Serve immediately, before the acidity of the dressing starts to wilt the leaves.

Monlar oo thoke | Pickled daikon salad with fried garlic

Sesame seeds and peanuts are grown in the hot central area of Burma and feature together in many of the dishes from this region. This refreshing salad with crisp textures and an intense blend of hot, sweet, salty, and sour flavors is characteristic of much of Southeast Asian cooking. It can be eaten as a starter or appetizer, but also works well as an accompaniment to other dishes.

Serves 4–6

3 tablespoons rice vinegar

1 teaspoon salt

1 teaspoon sugar

1 fresh red chile, seeded and finely chopped

1 large daikon (Japanese radish), about 1lb (450g), peeled

2 tablespoons skinned raw peanuts

1 tablespoon sesame seeds

3 tablespoons vegetable oil

6 garlic cloves, any inner green shoots removed, cut into slivers

3 scallions (green onions), finely sliced

handful of fresh cilantro leaves

1 tablespoon fish sauce such as nam pla

1 tablespoon garlic oil

Partner with
Malay fried noodles (p20)
Roast pork with fresh mint and peanuts (p159)

1 Put the vinegar, salt, and sugar in a large bowl. Stir together to dissolve the granules. Add the chile to the vinegar solution. Using a vegetable peeler, peel the daikon into thin ribbons. Toss in with the vinegar solution, and marinate in the refrigerator for 15 minutes.

2 Preheat the oven to 400°F (200°C). Spread the peanuts on a baking sheet, and roast in the oven for 4–5 minutes until golden brown. Remove the nuts to a cutting board and coarsely crush with the flat side of a knife. Set aside. Roast the sesame seeds in a dry frying pan over a medium-high heat for 2–3 minutes until they pop and are golden—be careful not to scorch them. Remove from the heat and also set aside.

3 Heat the vegetable oil in a small frying pan over a medium heat, and fry the garlic sliver for 1–2 minutes until crisp and golden brown. Using a slotted spoon, remove the garlic from the pan, and drain on paper towels. Reserve the oil for dressing the salad (or use good-quality bought garlic-infused olive oil if you prefer).

4 When ready to serve, remove the pickled daikon from the refrigerator, and drain off any excess liquid. Add the scallions, toasted sesame seeds, and crushed peanuts. Tear the cilantro into the salad. (It is important not to tear the cilantro leaves until you are actually adding them to the salad, as they will otherwise lose flavor and vitality.) Add half the fried garlic. Combine the fish sauce with 1 tablespoon of the garlic oil, and use to dress the salad. Garnish the salad with the remaining cilantro leaves and fried garlic slivers, and serve immediately.

Cho go chu jang | Sashimi of sea bass with hot dressing

Korea's location on a peninsula, surrounded by ocean waters, means that there is a bounty of fish and seafood in the Korean diet. Sashimi is a common way of eating fresh fish such as sea bass, but the condiments are different to those used in Japanese cuisine. Korean food is seen as medicine as well as sustenance, and so an ongoing balance is sought to achieve the right harmony between the body and the taste buds. As the fish will be eaten raw, make sure to let your fishmonger know that you want the freshest sushi-grade fish.

1 Ask your fishmonger to bone and skin the fish. Alternatively, do it yourself. To skin the fish, dip your finger and thumb into some salt, so you can get a good grip on the tail end of the fish—the salt will work as an abrasive. Using a thin knife, insert the blade down into the flesh near the tail end. Work your knife gently along so that the blade is horizontal to the skin, pointing away from you. Increase the tension in your thumb and finger holding the tail. Run the knife in long, smooth strokes from left to right away from you, running along and separating the skin from the flesh. At the same time, pull the skin toward you at the same speed as the knife, so that piece of fish is being worked into the path of knife in your other hand.

2 Finely slice the fish across the grain into thin slices. If not using immediately, cover and store the fish in the refrigerator until needed. With the back of a knife, work the garlic, pinch of salt, and sugar on a chopping board, to make a smooth pulp. Mix the crushed garlic with the kochujang in a bowl. Add the sesame oil, light soy sauce, and lemon juice, and mix together.

3 When ready to serve, gently lay the slices of fish on a serving platter. Season with black pepper, and scatter with the scallion. Pour the spicy sesame dressing over the fish and serve. The combination of hot, salty, and sour flavors in the dressing pairs brilliantly with the sweetness of the fresh fish.

Serves 4

1lb (450g) sea bass, snapper, or other similar fish

1 garlic clove, any inner green shoot removed, finely chopped

pinch of salt

1 teaspoon sugar

2 teaspoons kochujang (Korean chile bean paste)

3 tablespoons sesame oil

2 tablespoons light soy sauce

juice of 1 lemon

3 scallions (green onions), finely sliced

freshly ground black pepper

Partner with
Laotian spice-pickled scallions (pp168–9)
Sichuan peppered beef (pp170–1)

Yam som tam | Hot and sour green papaya salad

When I arrive in Thailand, this is always the first thing I eat. This salad epitomizes everything that is good about Thai food. You have all the elements of hot, sweet, salty, and sour present in every mouthful. The textures also combine to give your mouth a workout—there are crisp, crunchy, chewy, and soft all together. The colors are fresh, and so all your senses are stimulated. In the hot tropical humidity of Southern Thailand, this is the ultimate refreshment. Unripe papayas are hard and green-skinned; look for them in Asian produce markets.

Serves 4

1 large green unripe papaya

4 tablespoons skinned raw peanuts

3 garlic cloves, any inner green shoots removed, finely chopped

4 hot fresh bird's-eye chiles, seeded and finely chopped

pinch of salt

2 tablespoons small dried shrimp

1 tablespoon palm sugar or brown sugar

8 cherry tomatoes, cut into quarters

juice of 2 limes

2 tablespoons fish sauce such as nam pla

1 Peel the skin off the papaya and discard. Continue to peel the flesh into strips. Stack the strips on a chopping board, then use a knife to chop them into thin matchsticks. Dry-roast the peanuts in a heavy pan over a medium-high heat for 3–4 minutes until golden brown. Shake the pan frequently, and be careful not to scorch the peanuts. Remove from the heat and allow to cool.

2 Using a large mortar and pestle, pound the garlic, chile, and a pinch of salt to a paste. Add the dried shrimp and sugar, and continue to pound to break the shrimp down (as they are hard). Add the tomato and gently crush—be careful that it does not splash too much. Lastly, add the lime juice and fish sauce to make a dressing.

3 Pour the dressing over the green papaya. Using the mortar and pestle, lightly crush the roasted peanuts so that they are broken up. Sprinkle the crushed peanuts over the papaya. Toss the salad together, and serve immediately for a true taste sensation.

Partner with
Stir-fried beef with chile and onion relish (p33)
Burmese turmeric fishcakes (p80)

Tangy and refreshing

When many people think of Asian food, they think of heat, as in chiles. Yet there is another aspect of Asian food that should not be neglected, and that is those dishes that are almost an explosion of tang and flavor—a firework display for your taste buds. Tamarind, citrus, lemongrass, and lime leaves play a role in this, as well as other key ingredients in the Asian spice collection such as Sichuan pepper and turmeric. Chutneys, pickles, dipping sauces, and vegetable dips also demonstrate a concentration of flavor that is refreshing and enlivening.

Rendang daging | Malay beef rendang

A dish clearly showing the mix of cultures that influence Malaysian food, this dry beef curry has virtual cult status in Malaysia. The beef is slowly cooked so that the juices are absorbed and evaporate, leaving the meat meltingly soft—a cooking method also found in India. The flavorings of lime leaves, lemongrass, and galangal, however, mark rendang's foundations in Southeast Asia.

Serves 4–6

2 tablespoons vegetable oil

2lbs (750g) beef shin, trimmed and cut into ¾in (2cm) cubes

1½ quarts (1.5 litres) coconut cream

1 tablespoon tamarind pulp

1 teaspoon ground turmeric

5 kaffir lime leaves

a little freshly squeezed lime juice

salt and freshly ground black pepper

For the spice paste

8 fresh red chiles, seeded and finely chopped

10 shallots, finely chopped

4 garlic cloves, any green inner shoots removed, finely chopped

4 lemongrass stems, tougher outer layer removed, finely chopped

1¾in (4cm) piece of fresh ginger, finely chopped

2 teaspoons brown sugar

Partner with
Sumatran eggplant sambal (pp88–9)
Singapore coconut laksa (p112)

1 For the spice paste, put the chile, shallot, garlic, lemongrass and ginger in a food processor, and blend to a smooth paste. You may need to add a little coconut cream to keep the blade turning.

2 Heat a heavy pan over a medium-high heat. Add the oil, and fry the spice paste for 4–5 minutes until fragrant. Season the beef with salt and black pepper, and add to the spice paste, coating all the pieces for 2 more minutes. Add the coconut cream, tamarind pulp, turmeric, and whole lime leaves. Bring the mixture to the boil, then reduce the heat to low and simmer very gently.

3 Stir the meat every 10 minutes to keep it from sticking, and simmer until the liquid has almost evaporated and the meat is tender, at least 1½ hours. Add a little water if the liquid evaporates before the meat is tender. Continue cooking the beef until the sauce becomes thick and is almost dry. Be patient: this method of slow-cooking enhances the final flavor.

4 Taste the rich sauce. It will be hot and slightly sour, with an underlying sweetness from the coconut cream. Adjust the seasoning with salt and a little lime juice to balance the flavors. Although rendang is a dish that takes some time to cook, it is not complicated and definitely worth the wait. Serve as part of larger meal with rice and other accompanying dishes such as relishes, sambals, vegetable dishes, and noodles.

Batu sambol | Sri Lankan smoky eggplant dip

A similar method is used to make this dip as is found in the Middle Eastern *baba ghanoush*, where the eggplants are grilled whole over a flame. This cooks and softens the eggplants inside and imparts a smoky taste from the charred skin on the outside. Ground almonds enrich the overall flavor and texture.

1 Heat a broiler or a cast-iron ridged grill pan until very hot. Place the eggplants on a baking tray under the broiler or in the pan, and blacken all over, allowing 3–4 minutes on each side. Grill for a total of 12–15 minutes until the skin is charred and the flesh inside softened and cooked. Remove from the heat and allow to cool.

2 Heat the 2 tablespoons oil in a heavy pan over a medium-high heat. Sweat the onion for 5–7 minutes. Push the onion to one side of the pan, then add the chopped ginger, garlic, and chile. Fry the aromatics in the oil for 2 minutes until fragrant, then stir into the onion mixture. Reduce the heat to low.

3 Cut the softened eggplant in half lengthways, and scoop out the flesh and seeds. Discard the skin, and chop the flesh. Add the tomato purée, paprika, cinnamon, and cumin to the onion mixture, and cook over a low heat for 4–5 minutes until fragrant. Mix in the chopped eggplant flesh, and cook for a further 2 minutes to combine all the flavors. Stir in the ground almonds and chopped cilantro. Season well with salt and black pepper.

4 Transfer the mixture to a blender or food processor, and purée until smooth. While the motor is running, gradually add the extra 2½fl oz (75ml) olive oil in a thin, constant stream, as you would when making a mayonnaise. Pour in the lime juice and mix together. Check the seasoning. The dip will be hot from the chile and the spices, salty and smoky from the seasoning and grilling, sweet from the onion and the cooked eggplant, and sharpened by the lime juice. Add more salt, lime juice, or fresh chile if required, so that all the flavors are balanced. Serve with plenty of hot fresh bread as the start of a meal or use as a relish or condiment as part of a larger meal.

Serves 4–6

2 large eggplants

2 tablespoons olive oil, plus 2½fl oz (75ml) extra

1 onion, finely chopped

1¼in (3cm) piece of fresh ginger, finely chopped

2 garlic cloves, any green inner shoots removed, finely chopped

1 fresh red chile, seeded and finely chopped

1 teaspoon tomato purée

½ teaspoon paprika

1 teaspoon ground cinnamon

1 teaspoon ground cumin

1 tablespoon ground almonds

1 small bunch of fresh cilantro, leaves picked and chopped

juice of 1 lime

salt and freshly ground black pepper

Partner with
Seared scallops with fresh chutney (pp16–17)
Fried puffed potato bread (pp62–3)

Sichuan spicy pickled cucumber

Pickled vegetables are hugely popular in China and indeed throughout Asia. These intensely-flavored pickled cucumbers are usually eaten as a snack or at the beginning of the meal. Many hot pickle recipes use chile or chile oil for heat; this one uses some Sichuan pepper as well, which imparts a slight numbing sensation to the tongue.

Serves 6 as a snack

3 large cucumbers

½ teaspoon salt

2in (5cm) piece of fresh ginger

1 fresh red chile, seeded and finely chopped

3 tablespoons sesame oil

½ teaspoon Sichuan pepper

½ teaspoon crushed dried red chile flakes

2 tablespoons rice vinegar

1 tablespoon sugar

1 Cut the cucumbers in half lengthways, and remove the central core of seeds. Cut the cucumber flesh into 2½in x ¾in (6cm x 2cm) batons. Put the cucumber in a bowl, and sprinkle with the salt. Mix together and leave for 30 minutes.

2 Discard any water in the bowl that has accumulated from the cucumber. Lightly rinse the cucumber under cold running water, then pat dry with paper towels. Thinly slice the ginger, then finely shred. Put the cucumber in a clean bowl with the ginger and chopped red chile.

3 Heat a saucepan over medium-high heat, and add the sesame oil and Sichuan pepper. Cook for 15–30 seconds until fragrant. Add the crushed chile flakes and mix together, then pour the liquid over the cucumber. Toss together and leave to cool.

4 When the cucumber is cool, mix the vinegar with the sugar until dissolved. Add the vinegar mixture to the cucumber, and toss together to coat. Marinate for 2–6 hours—the longer it sits, the softer the cucumber will be. Serve as a snack or to accompany grilled meat dishes as part of a larger meal.

Partner with
Sesame chicken salad with white pepper (pp118–19)
Sichuan peppered beef (pp170–1)

Nuoc dau phung | Vietnamese peanut dipping sauce

From Indonesia to Vietnam, countless versions of peanut sauce can be found throughout Southeast Asia. This one is very light, not heavy and cloying, and allows you to taste all the ingredients. Try the peanut sauce with the happy crêpes on pp86–7, or as a condiment with grilled seafood, chicken, or meat.

1 Roast the peanuts for 3–4 minutes until golden brown. Coarsely chop 1 tablespoon of the nuts and crush the rest. Using the back of a knife, crush the garlic with a little salt on a chopping board.

2 Heat the oil in a heavy pan over a medium-high heat, and fry the garlic, chile, and ginger for 3–4 minutes until fragrant. Add the crushed peanuts (reserving the chopped ones to use later), reduce the heat, and cook for a further 3–4 minutes.

3 Add the water or chicken stock, sugar, fish sauce, and hoisin sauce, and bring to the boil. Reduce the heat and simmer for 12–15 minutes until the oil from the peanuts has risen to the surface. Remove from the heat and allow to cool, then add the lime juice and chopped peanuts. Transfer to a serving bowl for dipping.

Serves 6

3 tablespoons skinned raw peanuts

1 garlic clove

a little salt

1 tablespoon vegetable oil

1 small fresh bird's-eye chile, seeded and very finely chopped

1in (2cm) piece of fresh ginger, finely grated

½ cup water or chicken stock if available

4 tablespoons coconut cream

2 teaspoons sugar

1 tablespoon fish sauce such as nuoc nam

1 tablespoon hoisin sauce

juice of 1 lime

Partner with
Minced pork balls with garlic and pepper (pp38–9)
Happy crêpes (pp86–7)
Tamarind fried shrimp (pp154–5)

Asam udang | Tamarind fried shrimp

Tamarind is one of the hallmark ingredients of Southeast Asian and South Indian cuisines. With this simple and utterly delicious recipe, in one mouthful you enjoy a blend of the four major tastes—hot, sweet, salty, and sour. Use the marinade for fish or other shellfish, chicken, or pork.

Serves 4–6

2 tablespoons tamarind pulp
(see right)

1 tablespoon light soy sauce

½ teaspoon sugar

1 teaspoon crushed black pepper

½ teaspoon crushed dried red
chile flakes

1¼lbs (600g) raw shrimp, peeled
and deveined

2 tablespoons vegetable oil

salt

1 Mix together the tamarind pulp, soy sauce, sugar, pepper, and chile flakes in a bowl. Add the shrimp, cover, and marinate in the refrigerator for at least 1 hour, turning the shrimp two or three times to ensure that they are fully coated.

2 Season the shrimp with salt. Heat the oil in pan over a medium-high heat, and fry the shrimp until they are dark brown on both sides. These can be served as a starter with some cucumber slices or as part of large meal with a number of components.

Preparing tamarind Tamarind, a seed pod with a brown skin the color of cinnamon, grows on a shade tree of the same name widely found in South and Southeast Asia. The interior of a tamarind seed is sticky and meaty like a date, but with stringy membranes and hard pits. It is available in a number of different forms: as raw pods, as a cake that looks like a big bar of chocolate, or bought processed as tamarind pulp in a jar, which is by far the easiest form to work with. Tamarind is also available as a concentrate, which I think is too strong—it is very black and too overpowering in its concentration. If you are using the cake of pressed tamarind, place it in a large bowl and cover with hot water. Leave to soften for about an hour, then massage the flesh away from the pits and the stringy membranes, discarding both the pits and membranes. Add some more water to the tamarind paste to form a tamarind pulp. This pulp will keep in an airtight glass jar in the refrigerator for 1–2 weeks.

Partner with
Malay fried noodles (p20)
Grilled beef patties with
shallots and cumin (pp26–7)
Scallion pancakes (pp60–1)

Keynotes | **Preserved fish products**

The salty element of Asian cooking comes in many forms – fermented soybean products, such as soy sauce, tempeh, and bean paste, for instance. The other main area where salt is found is in dried and fermented fish products. The intense tropical humidity that exists across much of China and Southeast Asia, combined with a lack of proper refrigeration, means that fish and seafood spoil very easily if not eaten straight away. In the past, the only way to preserve much of it was to dry it in the sun,

salt it, or allow it ferment. These preservation methods are widely used across Southern China, Southeast Asia, Malaysia, and Indonesia. Salting and drying change the flavors from subtle to intense and powerful. As a result, dried and preserved seafood are seen more as condiments or flavorings, and used more sparingly than if fresh.

Dried seafood can be steamed, fried, or grilled, then used in combination with other, fresher ingredients. It includes fish, large, medium, and tiny; scallops; abalone; squid and cuttlefish; jellyfish; oysters; and shrimp.

Dried shrimp

These staple dried ingredients are widely used. In Thailand, Singapore, and Vietnam, stalls sell scores of different varieties. Every shade of orange and pink, ranging minutely in size, is represented, in open sacks like grain or rice. The smell of them on such a large scale is intensely pungent; they are best used in small portions. In China, dried shrimp appear in soups and rice dishes, and stuffed with minced pork in wonton dumplings. In Thailand, they are used in noodle dishes and pounded into salads such as the amazing *yam som tam*, hot and sour green papaya salads that originated from what is now Laos and have cult status all over Southeast Asia. In Malaysia, dried shrimp are crushed and added to spicy sambals. They can be steamed or soaked, lightly toasted, or simply crushed with garlic and chile using a mortar and pestle. When crushed, they lose their intense pungency, instead becoming aromatic and flavorful. Dried shrimp are best kept in airtight containers and can be bought from Chinese or Asian markets.

Shrimp paste

There are various forms of this pungent fermented paste across Southeast Asia. In Thailand it is called *kapi*, which is made by putting small shrimp into jars of salt and leaving them to ferment. The shrimp almost digest themselves as their digestive enzymes break down. In Malaysia, another version is made called *balacan*, a paste of pulverized shrimp and salt that is spread on a mat to dry in the sun. This paste is packed into bricks, then sold in smaller blocks or slices. Both are very pungent. When shrimp paste is wrapped in banana leaves or foil, and baked or dry-roasted for 5–10 minutes, the pungency disappears and the paste becomes aromatic. Blended with other flavors in curry pastes, marinades, dressings, and sambals, it imparts an intense depth of flavor with salty and savory characteristics, rather than fishy ones. *Sambal balacan* is a famous Malaysian paste of chiles, shrimp paste, lime leaves, and lime juice.

Fish sauce

Known as *nuoc nam* in Vietnam and *nam pla* in Thailand, fish sauce is essential to the cooking of Vietnam, Thailand, Burma, Cambodia, Laos, and the Philippines in the same way that soy sauce is to Chinese and Japanese cuisine. The aroma is stronger than the taste, and takes a bit of getting used to. Again, on its own it is strong and pungent; however, when combined with complementary elements such as lime juice, chiles, and fresh herbs, it is transformed. When cooked, it loses its fishy taste and adds depth of flavor instead.

Fish sauce is made by packing small anchovy-like fish in barrels of brine, which are left to ferment in the sun for a few months. The resulting brown liquid is highly nutritious. In Vietnam, there is a saying: "Without good fish sauce, food can never taste good, regardless of how talented the chef." This archetypal sauce is used to season food, as well being one of the main ingredients of the typical dipping sauces found in Southeast Asian cuisine. The best fish sauce comes from an island called Phu Quoc off the coast of Vietnam; the first run-off liquid is light amber and fragrant, and is best used for dipping sauces so that it is not cooked—rather like the finest extra virgin olive oil.

Shrimp paste

Fish sauce

Dried shrimp

"Salting and drying change the flavors from subtle to intense and powerful. As a result, dried and preserved seafood are seen more as condiments or flavorings."

Bun bi suon | Roast pork with fresh mint and peanuts

Two of the thrilling things about Southeast Asian food are the combination of different flavors in balance and the varying textures found in a single dish. This dish from Vietnam is no exception. The soft, chewy, and crisp textures of the pork, cucumber, and bean sprouts all seem to be exaggerated when put alongside crunchy peanuts.

1 Preheat the oven to 400°F (200°C). Place an ovenproof dish over a medium-high heat. Season the pork with salt and black pepper. When the dish is hot, add a little oil and the piece of pork. Seal the meat for 2 minutes on each side until it is browned. Transfer to the oven and roast for 20 minutes or until cooked. Remove from the oven and leave to cool.

2 While the pork is cooking, prepare the other ingredients. Spread the peanuts in a single layer on a roasting tray, and roast in the oven for 4–5 minutes until golden. Remove from the oven and allow the peanuts to cool, then coarsely crush using a mortar and pestle. Cut the cucumber into 2in (5cm) lengths. Cut thin vertical slices of the cucumber flesh, leaving the block of seeds in the centre untouched. (Discard the seeds because they are watery and not good for salads.) Rearrange the ribbons of cucumber into stacks, then cut into thin matchsticks. Cut the shallots in half and remove the tough core. Finely slice the shallots into wafer-thin slices. The accompanying spice-pickled scallions can be made in advance (see pp168–9).

3 To make the dressing, combine the chile, lime juice, and fish sauce in a small bowl. Add the sugar, and stir until dissolved. Remove the pork from the roasting tray, and transfer to a board for slicing. Pour some of the dressing into the roast pork pan, and use a wooden spoon to deglaze the pan—to pick up all the good bits and juices left by the roasting. Tip back into the rest of the dressing.

4 Slice the pork and mix with the cucumber, shallot, bean sprouts, and mint in a large bowl. Pour the dressing over the top, and toss together gently. Scatter over the peanuts, and serve with the spice-pickled scallions on the side.

Serves 4–6

2lbs (750g) pork tenderloin

vegetable oil for cooking

⅔–¾ cup skinned raw peanuts or cashews

1 cucumber

4 shallots

1lb (450g) bean sprouts, rinsed

handful of fresh mint leaves

1 recipe Laotian Spice-pickled Scallions (see pp168–9)

salt and freshly ground black pepper

For the dressing

2 fresh red chiles, seeded and finely chopped

juice of 2 limes

2 tablespoons fish sauce such as nuoc nam

1 teaspoon sugar

Partner with
Shrimp and chive spring rolls (pp72–3)
Fried bean sprouts and clams (pp94–5)

Chutni zardolu | Spicy apricot chutney

Ripe stone fruit are used in this delicious spicy chutney hailing from Afghanistan, to preserve the fruit for the winter months. You can use apricots, peaches, nectarines, or plums, or a combination of these. It can also be made with ripe tomatoes if you like. Adjust the chile and spice content to suit your taste. And remember that it is very easy to make a large quantity of this if you wish.

Makes two 1-pint (450g) jars

3¼lbs (1.5kg) ripe apricots

1 cup white wine vinegar

2 tablespoons sugar

1 tablespoon salt

1 tablespoon vegetable oil

1 tablespoon coriander seeds, roughly crushed

2 garlic cloves, any green inner shoots removed, finely chopped

2 hot fresh green chiles, seeded and finely chopped

1¾in (4cm) piece of fresh ginger, finely chopped

1 cinnamon stick

1 Preheat the oven to 400°F (200°C). Put the apricots in a high-sided roasting tray. Bake in the oven for about 20 minutes until softened but not watery. Remove from the oven, and leave until cool enough to handle. Methodically work from one end of the pan to the other, removing the pit from each apricot. Transfer the flesh to a board and chop with a large knife. Reserve the juices in the pan.

2 Bring the vinegar to the boil with the sugar and salt, and simmer for 5 minutes. Using a separate pan, heat the oil over a medium-high heat, and add the crushed coriander seeds, garlic, chile, ginger, and cinnamon stick. Cook for 2 minutes until fragrant. Add the reserved apricot juices, and simmer until reduced and syrupy.

3 Remove the vinegar mixture from the heat, and combine with the spicy syrup and the chopped apricot flesh. Mix together. Check and adjust the seasoning to suit your taste. The mixture will be hot from the chile, and sweet, salty, and sour from the vinegar. If bottling, pour into sterilized glass jars with tight-fitting lids. Seal the jars while the chutney is still hot so that the resulting steam creates a vacuum—this helps the chutney to keep better and prevents spoiling. Regardless of whether you are bottling or not, allow 24 hours before using, to let the flavors combine and mellow.

Partner with

Garlic and cilantro naan (p49)

Gujarati aubergine fritters (pp82–3)

Pachadi | Carrot pachadi

A superb creation from Kerala in South India comprising a great combination of flavors and textures, *pachadi* is often served with warm *dosai* and other traditional flat breads. It can be made in advance and served either warm or at room temperature. *Pachadi* also works well as part of a large Asian meal.

1 Combine the grated carrot, shallot, and chile in a bowl, and add the salt. Mix thoroughly and set aside. Using a mortar and pestle, crush together the cumin seeds, cardamom pods, and half the mustard seeds. Discard the husks from the cardamom. Add the coconut, and pound to a rough paste.

2 Heat the oil in a large heavy pan over a medium-high heat, and fry the remaining mustard seeds for 20–30 seconds until they pop. Add the coconut mixture and fry for 2 minutes, stirring to prevent it catching. Next, add the carrot mixture. Stir-fry for another 1–2 minutes, tossing the mixture all the time.

3 Transfer to a bowl and allow to cool. Once cooled, add the yogurt and lemon juice, and mix together. Taste the mixture and season well with salt and black pepper, and a little extra red chile to suit your taste. You will get a great combination of hot from the chile, sweet from the carrot, sour from the lemon, and salty from the seasoning. Serve as individual bites in mini popadums, or alternatively pile into a large bowl and serve with flat breads such as *dosai* or garlic and cilantro naan (see p49).

Serves 4–6

4 carrots, grated

4 shallots, finely sliced

1 fresh red chile, seeded and finely chopped

½ teaspoon salt

1 teaspoon cumin seeds

2 green cardamom pods

2 teaspoons brown mustard seeds

1¾ cups shredded coconut

1 tablespoon oil

3 tablespoons Greek-style yogurt

juice of 1 lemon

salt and freshly ground black pepper

mini popadums, to serve

Partner with
Keralan spiced chickpea and lentil dumplings (pp56–7)
Potato with turmeric and mustard seeds (pp174–5)

Kimch'i | Korean hot pickled cabbage

Kimchee is an ancient method of preserving vegetables that has become a Korean staple. There are hundreds of different types, many of them featuring lots of garlic and chile. It can be preserved for a long time and provides vital vitamins and minerals that are otherwise missing in the Korean winter diet. A great condiment that can be eaten with rich grilled and roasted meats, or as part of soups or a stir-fry, kimchee is not difficult to make, but the process does extend over a couple of days.

Serves 6–8

1 long Chinese cabbage (napa cabbage)

½ cup (100g) coarse salt

1 teaspoon sugar

2½ teaspoons chile powder

1 daikon (Japanese white radish), cut into 1¾in (4cm) julienne

3 scallions, cut into 1¾in (4cm) julienne

4 garlic cloves, any green inner shoots removed, finely chopped

1¾in (4cm) piece of fresh ginger, finely chopped

1 tablespoon salted anchovies, finely chopped (optional)

1 Trim the root end of the cabbage, but do not cut or separate the leaves. Put about ⅓ cup of the salt into a large bowl, and add 4 cups (1 quart) water. Stir to dissolve the salt. Add the cabbage to the bowl, bending it so that it fits and is submerged. Add a little extra water if necessary so that the cabbage is covered. Place a plate over the top, and weight down so that the cabbage is covered in the salted water. Leave at room temperature for 12 hours until the cabbage has softened.

2 Mix the sugar with the chile powder and remaining salt. Combine with the daikon, scallion, garlic, ginger, and anchovy (if using). Sterilize a large sealable bell jar or similar in boiling water. Drain the cabbage and rinse well under cold running water. Squeeze the cabbage dry of excess water. Put the cabbage in a bowl, and gently separate the leaves, pushing spoonfuls of the spicy daikon mixture between each leaf to fill the gaps. Press the filled cabbage into the bell jar, pushing down to remove any pockets of air, then seal the jar tightly.

3 The jar of cabbage now needs to be left out of the refrigerator in a warm place (78°F/25°C) for 24 hours, to allow the cabbage to ferment. At the end of this time, transfer to the refrigerator and use as required. This spicy fermented condiment is chopped before serving and eaten cold. Serve with rich grilled or roasted meats such as *bulgogi* (see pp52–3).

Partner with
Stir-fried bean sprouts with chile bean paste (p21)
Marinated barbecue beef (pp52–3)

Imam bayildi | Spiced stuffed eggplant

The name of this very famous dish, with its many variations, translates as the "imam fainted." There are two versions as to why he did. The first is that he collapsed in rapturous delight when his wife made the dish for him. The second version says that he fainted when he discovered how much of his expensive olive oil had been used.

1 Preheat the oven to 400°F (200°C). Score the tomatoes with a sharp knife. Blanch in boiling water for 10 seconds, then refresh in cold water. Remove the skin, then cut the tomatoes in half and remove the seeds. Cut the flesh into a fine dice. Set aside.

2 Heat some of the oil in a large heavy pan. Fry the diced eggplant in small batches for 3–4 minutes until golden brown on all sides, then drain on paper towels. Cook in small batches so that the oil remains hot and the eggplant fries, rather than stews.

3 Put the garlic, cumin, coriander, and cayenne in the same pan used for the eggplant; fry for about 2 minutes until fragrant. Add the onion, reduce the heat, and sweat for 4 minutes until softened. Add the currants and remove from the heat. Stir in the fried diced aubergine and diced tomato. Sprinkle over the parsley and mix together. Season well with salt and black pepper.

4 Trim the caps from the whole eggplants, then peel off ½in (1cm) strips of skin with a very sharp knife, leaving alternate stripes of skin and bare flesh. Cut a long, deep slit down the centre of each eggplant—not all the way through. Using a spoon to push open the slit, stuff the pocket with the spiced eggplant mixture.

5 Pack the eggplants tightly into a baking dish so that they are side by side. Combine the passata with the sugar, lemon juice, the remaining olive oil and some salt. Pour over the eggplants. Spoon any leftover filling into the gaps around the dish. Cover the dish with aluminum foil, and bake in the oven for 45–60 minutes until the eggplant has softened and the sauce has reduced. Serve at room temperature with yogurt and lots of fresh bread.

Serves 4–6

⅔ cup olive oil

4 whole eggplants (preferably a small elongated variety such as Japanese eggplant)

1 cup passata

1 teaspoon sugar

juice of 1 lemon

Greek yogurt, to serve

For the filling

4 ripe tomatoes

2 eggplants, cut into ½in (1cm) dice

4 garlic cloves, any green inner shoots removed, finely chopped

1 tablespoon ground cumin

1 tablespoon ground coriander

½ teaspoon cayenne

2 onions, finely diced

⅔ cup currants

1 bunch of fresh flat-leaf parsley, leaves picked and chopped

salt and freshly ground black pepper

Partner with
Potato and cauliflower pakoras (pp66–7)
Spicy lamb-stuffed pancakes (p74)

Laotian spice-pickled scallions

Laos is sandwiched between Thailand and Vietnam, and employs the same principles of balancing flavors as its neighbors. Its cuisine is a blend of hot, sweet, salty, and sour, and leans to the spicier, robust, and fragrant end of the spectrum. Many favorite Southeast Asian dishes originated from Laos, such as the hot and sour green papaya salad called *yam som tam* in Thailand. I have had variations of these deliciously addictive pickled scallions in Vietnam as well.

Serves 4

3 bunches of scallions (green onions)

2 small dried chiles, crushed

1 tablespoon coriander seeds

½ cup rice vinegar

juice of 1 lime

1 teaspoon salt

2 teaspoons sugar

1 fresh red chile, seeded and finely chopped

2 bay leaves

4 star anise

1 Trim the scallions and, from the white end, cut into ¾in (2cm) lengths. Only cut the white and pale part of the scallions, which are the firmest part. When the stem starts to become darker green, stop slicing and set the rest of the scallions aside (these green lengths can be used for another dish). Using a mortar and pestle, or a spice grinder, crush the dried chile and coriander seeds.

2 Combine the vinegar, lime juice, salt, sugar, chile, bay leaves, and star anise in a small saucepan. Bring the mixture to the boil, then simmer over a medium heat for 2 minutes. Remove from the heat, and add the scallions. Let stand for 3 minutes. Remove the scallions from the hot vinegar using a slotted spoon, and transfer them to a bowl. Do not overcook the scallions; they will become too soft and fall apart.

3 Allow the vinegar mixture to cool completely. When cold, pour back over the scallions. These pickled scallions should be quite firm and have a great balance of the four main tastes. Enjoy them as a snack or as an accompaniment to grilled meat dishes or crispy salads with bean sprouts and roasted peanuts.

Partner with
Crisp cabbage salad with peanuts (pp134–5)
Roast pork with fresh mint and peanuts (pp158–9)

Hei jiao niu rou | Sichuan peppered beef

Using a significant amount of pepper brings out the inherent sweet, rich flavors of beef. Both black and Sichuan peppercorns appear in this dish, imparting a spiciness that goes well with the meat. Cooking a steak or piece of beef with salt and pepper will mean that the meat is sweeter than if you cooked it without that seasoning. The pepper draws out the sweetness in the same way that salt draws out liquid.

1 Heat enough oil for deep-frying in a wok or high-sided frying pan over a high heat. Using a mortar and pestle, crush the black and Sichuan peppercorns together. Put the cubes of meat in a bowl, and add 1 tablespoon water and the rice wine. Season with the ½ teaspoon salt and some black pepper. Massage the meat with both hands for about 1 minute until the meat absorbs the liquid.

2 Quickly deep-fry the beef in two batches, cooking each batch for 40 seconds. Drain the cubes of meat on paper towels and set aside. Pour all but 1 teaspoon of the oil into a metal bowl and let cool. Reheat the wok and stir-fry the garlic for 30 seconds, then add the crushed black peppercorns and Sichuan pepper. Stir-fry for 10 seconds, then add the beef, oyster sauce, soy sauce, and sesame oil. Stir-fry for a few seconds more so that all the beef is coated with sauce and the crushed pepper.

3 Take a cube of beef and some shredded lettuce, and wrap in a length of sliced cucumber. Repeat the process until all the beef has been used. Serve immediately. The cool, soothing lettuce and cucumber counteract the spiciness of the meat. Alternatively, serve the beef as a whole dish, without the lettuce and cucumber, with a selection of other dishes or perhaps noodles or rice.

Serves 4–6 as part of larger meal
vegetable oil for deep-frying
2 teaspoons black peppercorns
1 teaspoon Sichuan peppercorns
1lb (450g) beef fillet, trimmed and cut into 1in (2.5cm) cubes
2 tablespoon rice wine
½ teaspoon salt
3 garlic cloves, any green inner shoots removed, finely chopped
2 teaspoons oyster sauce
2 teaspoons light soy sauce
1 teaspoon sesame oil
freshly ground black pepper
shredded lettuce, to serve
cucumber, thinly sliced lengthways, to serve

Partner with
Stir-fried greens with garlic (pp18–19)
Steamed shrimp wontons (pp98–9)

Joojeh kabab | Lemon and saffron chicken kebabs

There is nothing complicated about this impressive Iranian dish with its blindingly simple marinade; the key is in the mat marinate the chicken for at least three hours or preferably overnight. Ideally, use small baby chickens, or poussins, which are very tender, or you could use chicken pieces such as thighs, breasts, and drumsticks, halved and with the skin on and bone left in.

Serves 4

4 skinless boneless chicken breasts, cut into large cubes or strips, or 4 baby chickens (poussins)

2 onions

juice of 2 lemons

½ teaspoon cayenne or paprika

1 teaspoon saffron threads

salt and freshly ground black pepper

chopped fresh flat-leaf parsley, to garnish

lemon wedges, to serve

1 If using baby chickens, take one and turn it over so that the back is exposed. Using a pair of kitchen scissors, cut down one side of the backbone from end to end. Repeat with the other side, removing the bone section, which is almost triangular in shape. With the backbone removed, place the chicken on a chopping board breast-side up. Using the side of a large kitchen knife, press down on the bird with the knife, flattening the flesh and the remaining bones at the back. Repeat with all the birds that you are cooking.

2 For each bird, take a skewer and pin the thigh to the wing section on each side. If you are using halved chicken pieces or cubes or strips of chicken, thread the meat (weave the strips, if using) onto several metal skewers to form kebabs. If you are using bamboo skewers, soak them in water for 20–30 minutes first.

3 Place the skewered chicken in a large shallow dish. Grate the onion onto the flesh. Pour the lemon juice over the chicken, and scatter with plenty of black pepper and cayenne. Rub the marinade all over the meat, and marinate in the refrigerator for at least 3 hours, or preferably overnight, turning regularly.

4 When ready to cook, heat a barbecue and allow the coals to die down and become white. Or, if using a ridged cast-iron grill pan, heat the pan until very hot. Remove the chicken from the marinade, and place the skewers on the grill. Add the saffron to the marinade, and season well with salt. Gently grill the chicken, basting constantly with the saffron marinade. Continue to turn and baste until the meat is tender. Serve scattered with chopped parsley and lemon wedges.

Partner with
Turkish zucchini fritters (p64)
Spiced stuffed eggplant (p165)
Saffron ice cream (pp210–11)

Aloo chaat | Potato with turmeric and mustard seeds

Savory potatoes such as this are often served as a filling for *dosai* or other breads, such as *puri* (see pp62–3) or *paratha*. Singapore has a large Indian population, and the dishes from this community are popular throughout the region. You will find a similar dish in Sri Lanka and India, as well as Pakistan and Central Asian countries. This makes a tasty accompaniment to a larger meal consisting of numerous dishes.

Serves 4–6

1lb (450g) potatoes, such as Yukon Gold

2 teaspoons coriander seeds

2 tablespoons oil

1 teaspoon brown mustard seeds

1 onion, finely chopped

½ teaspoon ground turmeric

½ teaspoon red chile powder

4 scallions (green onions), finely sliced

juice of 1 lemon

handful of fresh cilantro leaves

sprinkle of dried red chile flakes (optional)

salt and freshly ground black pepper

1 Boil the potatoes whole in a large pot of salted water until cooked, but still firm when the point of a knife is inserted. Drain and, when cool enough to handle, peel and cut the potatoes into ½in (1cm) cubes. Set aside.

2 Using a mortar and pestle, coarsely crush the coriander seeds. Heat the oil in a heavy pan over a medium-high heat. Add the mustard seeds and crushed coriander seeds. Fry for 30 seconds or so until the mustard seeds start to pop.

3 Add the onion to the pan, and reduce the heat to low. Gently sauté the onion for 5 minutes until soft and a pale golden color. Add the turmeric and chile powder, and stir to combine. Season well with salt and black pepper.

4 Add the diced potato, and fry for a couple of minutes until hot and all the flavors have combined. Add the scallion and lemon juice, and finish with the cilantro leaves. Add more salt or perhaps some dried red chile flakes to suit your taste. Serve immediately.

Partner with
Spicy green beans with chile (pp30–1)
Fried puffed potato bread (pp62–3)

Keynotes | **Citrus and lemongrass**

The fresh clean citrus zing that makes your tongue tingle is a vital characteristic of Asian food. It can be as simple as a wedge of lemon or lime with some grilled shrimp or more complex, in the form of lemongrass and lime leaves with the addition of tamarind. In whatever form, the sour citrus notes are essential not because they have a nice flavor (although this is true), but because when combined with the other strong flavors in Asian cuisine they bring everything into balance. In Thai cooking, this is called *rot chart*, or "correct taste." The opposite of hot is sweet because the acid in chiles is soluble in sugar, not water. This is why, when you have something that is too hot or spicy, you should cool it with yogurt, cucumber, or honey, or something sweet. The opposite of salty is sour. When these four elements are combined, there is a perfect balance of flavor and the food is delicious.

The role of citrus

Citrus cuts through the fattiness and richness of foods such as roast pork or coconut cream. It also refreshes and enlivens any dish, forming contrasts between ingredients. A squeeze of citrus at the end of cooking works much like a highlighter pen on a page of writing. It draws attention to certain elements and helps them to stand out—it makes other ingredients work harder.

Kaffir lime leaves

Kaffir limes

Lemongrass

Lime juice

Lemons and limes (*Citrus* spp.) are probably the most widely used citrus fruits in the world. Lemons originated in India and were brought to Europe by the Romans in the 1st century AD. These fruits have

"Citrus notes are essential not because they have a nice flavor (although this is true), but because when combined with the other strong flavors in Asian cuisine they bring everything into balance."

been used as food and medicine in Asia for thousands of years. They both work as the perfect natural flavor enhancer. If something you are cooking is overseasoned and too salty, add a squeeze of lemon or lime juice to readjust the balance and counter the saltiness.

Both the zest and the juice can be used in many different styles of dish. The zest provides all the vibrancy, but with none of the acid. When you are zesting citrus, it is important that you zest only the thin colored part of the skin that contains all the citrus oils, not the bitter thick white pith. Also, to maximize the amount of juice from a tough lemon or lime, roll the fruit firmly under your hand on a board with your weight on top. This breaks down the fibers inside, resulting in more juice.

Lemongrass

Lemongrass (*Cymbopogon citratus*) is mostly used in Thai and Vietnamese cuisine, and some Malay and Indonesian food. This highly perfumed reed-like plant is native to Southeast Asia and has an amazing lemony perfume, but without the acidity of citrus.

Fresh lime

Lemongrass is used in a number of ways. The tough stalk is pounded and bruised to release the aromas, then cooked whole to impart a huge burst of flavor as in *tom yam* (hot and sour soup).

Alternatively, the tough outer layers of the stalk are removed, leaving the more tender stem inside. This is finely chopped into thin rounds and added to salads and garnishes. It must be cut very finely; if too thick, it would be like chewing a stick.

In Southeast Asia, the flavorful stems are also used as skewers, to impart their unique aroma. Lemongrass also features as one of the main ingredients of Thai curry pastes and marinades.

Kaffir limes

Kaffir limes (*Citrus hystrix*) are often called fragrant limes or makrut limes, and look quite unusual compared to regular limes. The skin is dark green and very knobbly. Both skin and the fragrance of the juice are very intense, reminiscent of a citric essence or the most expensive type of perfume. These have far less juice than ordinary limes, but a little goes a long way. Kaffir lime zest can be grated into curry pastes, marinades, and herb dressings. The zest can also be frozen for later use. If kaffir limes are not available, double the amount of regular limes.

The kaffir lime tree also produces a fragrant dark green leaf that is common in the Southeast Asian larder. Used whole in soups and curries, or finely shredded as a garnish and marinade ingredient, the leaves are best kept in a sealed bag in the freezer to hold their color and prevent them from drying out. The leaves defrost in seconds and can then be finely chopped or shredded, or used whole to flavor sauces.

Kai ge | Fried eggplant with toasted sesame seeds

With a Korean meal, many small dishes come to the table at the same time. Some are hot; some are served cold. Others are vegetables or condiments with varying textures and tastes. One dish may be highly spiced, such as kimchee (p164), while another may have no spice or be lightly pickled. Enjoy this eggplant dish with sesame seeds hot or cold, or combine it with ingredients to make a more substantial salad.

Serves 6

4 eggplants

3 tablespoons salt

2in (5cm) piece of fresh ginger, cut into thin matchsticks

2 tablespoons light soy sauce

1 tablespoon sesame oil

1 tablespoon rice vinegar

olive oil for frying

3 garlic cloves, any green inner shoots removed, finely chopped

¾ cup sesame seeds

juice of 1 lime

salt and freshly ground black pepper

Partner with
Marinated barbecue beef (pp52–3)
Steamed green vegetable rolls (p105)

1 Cut the eggplants into 1in (2cm) cubes and place in a large colander. Sprinkle the 3 tablespoons salt on the eggplant, and mix together to coat. Leave to drain for 30 minutes. This process removes the bitterness and some excess water. Meanwhile, prepare the other ingredients. Finely slice the ginger, then restack the pieces and cut into a fine needle-like shred. Mix together the light soy sauce, sesame oil, and rice vinegar in a small bowl.

2 After 30 minutes, rinse the eggplant under cold water to wash off the bitter liquid and the salt. Shake off any excess water while the eggplant is still in the colander, then thoroughly pat the eggplant dry with paper towels.

3 Heat 3–4 tablespoons olive oil in a heavy pan over a medium-high heat. In three or four batches, fry the eggplant until it is lightly golden brown on all sides. Fry in small batches so that the temperature of the oil does not drop—this ensures that the eggplant fries, rather than stews. When cooked, remove the eggplant from the pan with a slotted spoon, and drain on paper towels. Add a little more olive oil between each batch if necessary.

4 When all the eggplant is cooked, fry the garlic and sesame seeds until golden brown. Return the eggplant to the pan together with the ginger, and mix together. Add the soy and sesame liquid, and stir through. Season well with salt and black pepper, and pour over the lime juice. Taste the eggplant and adjust the seasoning to suit your taste. The dish should be sweet, salty, sour, and well seasoned. Eat hot or cold.

Tamatar chatni | Tomato chutney with green chile

Smooth and spicy, this tomato relish goes well with freshly grilled fish or chicken, or as an accompaniment to vegetable dishes. It is simple to make, and it is also very easy to increase the quantities of the ingredients to make a larger batch. This way you can keep some in sterilized jars in the refrigerator for use whenever you fancy. Or you might like to give it away as gifts—if you can bear to part with it.

1 Cut the tomatoes in half. Using a box grater, grate the flesh into a bowl, holding the skin side of the tomatoes in the palm of your hand. This is a quick way of getting tomato pulp, and the skin stays in your hand to be discarded when you are finished. Set aside.

2 Heat the oil in a heavy pan over a medium-high heat. Fry the garlic for 2 minutes until fragrant, then add the onion and reduce the heat. Cook down slowly for 5 minutes until softened. Add the ground cumin and turmeric to the pan; cook for 1 minute to allow the flavors to combine before adding the green chile. Stir together, then add the tomato pulp. Season with the salt and some black pepper, and simmer slowly for 5 minutes until everything is well blended and the tomato liquid has cooked off.

3 Transfer the mixture to a blender or food processor, add the lemon juice, and purée until smooth. Taste and adjust the seasoning. If the tomatoes are a bit too sour, sprinkle in the brown sugar and stir through. The chutney will be hot from the chile, sweet from the onion (and sugar), and salty and sour from the lemon juice. Divide the chutney between two 1-pint canning jars. Let cool, refrigerate, and use within one month.

Makes 2 pints (2 x 450g jars)

8 tomatoes

1 tablespoon vegetable oil

6 garlic cloves, any green inner shoots removed, finely chopped

2 onions, finely chopped

1 teaspoon ground cumin

1 teaspoon ground turmeric

2 fresh green chiles, seeded and finely chopped

½ teaspoon salt

juice of 1 lemon

1 teaspoon brown sugar (optional)

freshly ground black pepper

Partner with
Isaan-style grilled chicken (pp40–1)
Rice flour pancakes (p81)
Carrot pachadi (pp162–3)

Trai me thit bo | Tamarind beef with peanuts

I was served this very effective beef dish when I was a guest at someone's home in Vietnam while making a TV series about the country's vibrant food. It is strikingly different because of the tamarind caramel and the semi-pickled onion. There may seem to be a lot of sugar, but it is well balanced by the tamarind and vinegar. Use a tender cut of beef that can be cooked very quickly, or substitute chicken or pork.

Serves 4–6

1 lb (450g) top round, thinly sliced

2 teaspoons fish sauce such as nuoc nam

2 teaspoons light soy sauce

2 tablespoons tamarind pulp (see p154)

2 tablespoons vegetable oil

2 garlic cloves, any green inner shoots removed, minced

4 teaspoons white sugar

⅔ cup skinned raw peanuts

1 onion, finely sliced

2 tablespoons rice wine vinegar

small handful of fresh cilantro leaves, roughly chopped

small handful of fresh mint leaves, roughly chopped

small handful of arugula, mustard leaves, or watercress, or a mixture, roughly chopped

salt and freshly ground black pepper

1 Put the beef in a glass or ceramic dish or bowl. Season well with black pepper. Combine the fish sauce and soy sauce, pour over the beef, and marinate in the refrigerator for 30 minutes.

2 Dissolve the tamarind pulp in ¼ cup water. Heat half the oil in a heavy pan over a medium-high heat. Fry the garlic for about 2 minutes until golden brown, then add the tamarind liquid and half the sugar. Reduce the heat to medium, and continue to cook until the liquid reduces to a thick syrup the consistency of honey.

3 Roast the peanuts in a dry frying pan until golden brown, taking care not to scorch them. Remove from the heat and allow to cool, then coarsely chop and set aside. Put the onion in a bowl with the vinegar and remaining sugar. Season with salt, and mix together to semi-pickle the onions. Heat the remaining oil in a clean pan. Stir-fry the slices of marinated beef in small batches until golden brown, then set aside.

4 Quickly toss together the cilantro, mint, and other leaves, and arrange in a layer over the bottom of a shallow serving dish. Spoon the semi-pickled onion over the top, adding all the juices. Place the beef on top of the onion. Alternatively, arrange in small individual bowls or glasses. Pour on the caramelized tamarind syrup, garnish with the peanuts, and serve.

Partner with
Sumatran duck sate (pp50–1)
Burmese spiced split pea fritters (pp90–1)

Sugar and **spice**

Sweet treats in Asia range from fresh tropical fruit and thirst-quenching drinks, through to more elaborate cakes, pastries, and puddings featuring spices and nuts. Often, the perfect end to a meal of hot, spicy dishes is simply a fresh fruit salad or a cooling citrus or coconut dessert. There are other times, however, when a rich saffron ice cream or perhaps crisply battered pears drenched in scented honey syrup is the order of the day. And there is no need to limit your enjoyment to mealtimes. Pastries and cakes make great snacks at any time.

Woon ma praw orn | Citrus and young coconut jelly

One layer in this striking-looking gelatine dish is clear with citrus zest suspended in it, while the other layer is made from coconut cream with suspended pieces of coconut. For visual appeal, make it in small clear shot glasses, or prepare it in a flat tray, then cut into squares or diamond shapes.

Serves 8

1 cup coconut water (the liquid from the packet of frozen young coconut)

1 tablespoon (15g) powdered agar agar

pinch of salt

1 cup superfine sugar

1 package young coconut meat, shredded (available from the freezer section of Chinese, Thai, and Asian markets)

2 cups coconut cream

grated zest of 1 orange

grated zest of 1 lemon

fresh jasmine flowers (optional) (see note)

1 Combine the young coconut liquid with 3½ cups water. Pour into a saucepan. Stir in the agar agar. Bring the liquid to a simmer, and continue to simmer for 10 minutes. Add a pinch of salt and the sugar, and stir to dissolve. Remove from the heat. Mix the shredded young coconut meat with the coconut cream. Mix in half the reduced sugar water. Warm in a separate pan, but do not allow to boil.

2 Add the orange and lemon zests to the second half of the sugar water. Leave to cool. The orange color of the zest will leach into the water. (Lime zest and lemon zest could be added instead, to alter color and flavor.) Taste the two liquids. The salt will work to bring out the flavor of the coconut.

3 The two liquids will start to set as they cool, much more quickly than if gelatine had been used. Quickly but carefully pour the coconut cream and meat into clean molds, shot glasses, or a flat tray. Leave a space at the top for the clear orange jelly.

4 Once the white coconut jelly starts to set and can hold the other liquid, carefully pour the clear orange jelly over the top. Set in the refrigerator for 1–2 hours before turning out. The orange jelly could be poured in the first, to reverse the colors. Be careful if you choose to do this because the white coconut jelly is heavier. Serve with tropical Asian fruits, if liked.

Note Unsprayed jasmine flowers can be warmed in the sugar syrup and set in the citrus jelly, for decoration. If agar agar is not available, substitute gelatine. Do not set the jelly so hard that it is rubbery.

Partner with
North Vietnamese fish brochettes (pp46–7)
Mangosteen, lychee, and mango salad (p208)

Yogurtlu samfistigi kek | Yogurt and pistachio cake

Variations of yogurt and nut cake abound throughout the Levant and Middle East, and have been made for centuries. This particular one originates from Turkey. When paired with bright colored fruits such as pomegranate or roasted quince, it takes on a regal elegance. This would not have been out of place at a palace feast in the once-opulent Persian empire. You can bake the large version of this cake in advance, even the night before, but individual cupcakes should be eaten freshly made.

1 Preheat the oven to 350°F (180°C). Lightly grease and flour a standard muffin pan or friand pan. If making one large cake, lightly grease and flour an 8–10in (20–25cm) springform cake pan.

2 Grind the pistachio nuts and walnuts in a food processor (you can leave some in slightly bigger chunks to add some texture to the cake). Sift the flour with the baking soda, baking powder, and salt. Add the orange and lemon zest.

3 Beat the egg yolks with half the sugar with an electric mixer until pale and thick. Mix in the yogurt and olive oil, then fold in the ground nuts and flour mixture. In a separate bowl, beat the egg whites with the cream of tartar until they form soft peaks. Pour the remaining sugar into the egg whites, and continue to beat until the egg whites are stiff and glossy, and hold their shape.

4 Using a rubber spatula, gently fold the egg whites into the batter. Divide the batter among the prepared pans or pan. Bake in the center of the oven for 20 minutes if making individual cupcakes or 55 minutes if using a single large pan—the top of the cake should be springy to the touch if pressed lightly with your finger. Remove the pan from the oven and sit on a wire rack. Allow to cool in the pan, then turn out and dust with confectioners' sugar before serving with the fresh pomegranate seeds, if using.

Serves 6

1–1¼ cups (125g) skinned pistachio nuts

¼ cup walnuts

1¼ cups all-purpose flour

½ teaspoon baking soda

½ teaspoon baking powder

½ teaspoon salt

grated zest of 1 orange

grated zest of 1 lemon

6 eggs, separated

1 cup sugar

150g (5oz) Greek-style yogurt

½ cup olive oil

½ teaspoon cream of tartar

confectioners' sugar, to dust

fresh pomegranate seeds, to serve (optional)

Partner with
Spicy lamb-stuffed pancakes (p74)
Afghan caramelized quince compote (p191)

Keynotes | **Nuts and seeds**

Asian cuisine abounds with dishes featuring nuts and seeds. Nuts have a large percentage of oil and are also high in protein, so they are very important in the Asian diet. Ground nuts and sesame seeds are

> "Ground nuts and sesame seeds are used in condiments, sauces, soups, salads, and sambals not only for the texture and body that they provide, but also for their nutritional value."

used in condiments, sauces, soups, salads, and sambals not only for the texture and body that they provide, but also for their nutritional value.

Sesame seeds

Sesame seeds (*Sesamum indicum*) are available in both white and black varieties. In cultivation since 3000 BC, they originated in India and soon traveled to Assyria in Central Asia, as well as to East Africa, and have been used in China for at least 2,000 years. Sesame seeds are used widely in Middle Eastern, Southeast Asian, and Chinese kitchens. They are crushed in pastes and made into oils, as well as eaten raw and toasted. In North and Western China, a sesame paste similar to the Middle Eastern tahini is made with toasted seeds.

Sesame oil can vary from pale golden to dark rich brown, depending on whether the sesame seeds are toasted or the oils blended. The blended toasted oil gives an aromatic quality to marinades and dressings, but should be used sparingly so that it does not overpower the food.

An introduced favourite

The cashew is actually the fruit of a small tree, *Anacardium occidentale*, which is a member of the Anacardiaceae family, along with the mango, pistachio, poison ivy, and poison oak. Cashews are native to northeastern Brazil. The Portuguese introduced cashews to the west coast of India and East Africa in the 16th century, shortly after they first found it in 1578. After the cashew's planting in India, more-refined methods for removing the caustic shell oil were developed by this country, and India is given credit for developing the modern

Pistachio nuts

Pistacia vera are native to Western Asia and Asia Minor, from Syria to the Caucasus and Afghanistan. Archaeological evidence in Turkey indicates the nuts were being used for food as early as 7,000 BC. Pistachio nuts cannot tolerate excessive dampness and humidity, so, although they are used extensively in Western Asia, and parts of Central Asia, Pakistan, and India, they are not used at all in Eastern and Southeast Asia. Pistachios are prized for their ornamental color and flavor. They are used both raw and roasted, and can be salted or used in desserts such as baklava and similar pastries common throughout the Middle East, Western Asia, and what was once Persia. The bright green color bewitches the eye, creating jeweled dishes the like of which has been used to impress royalty for millennia.

nut industry. Cashews are now a high-yielding cash crop grown in many countries. Vietnam grows 28 per cent of the world's crop, and India still grows 25 per cent. On India's west and south coasts, cashews are used in pilafs, curries, and desserts, as well as chutneys. Ground cashews are used to thicken and enrich curries traditionally served at weddings, banquets, and other sumptuous occasions. Cashews are also used in Chinese and Malaysian cooking, but are usually left whole.

Cashews

the Malay archipelago, from where they quickly spread throughout Asia. In Asia, peanuts are much more than a snack food. They are nutritious and contain valuable vitamin E, niacin, folacin, calcium, phosphorus, magnesium, zinc, iron, riboflavin, thiamine, and potassium.

Peanuts

More than a snack food

Although peanuts (*Arachis hypogaea*) are considered to be nuts culinary-wise, botanically they belong to the legume family Fabaceae, which includes lentils, soybeans, and peas. Peanuts originated in South America; archaeological evidence shows that they were cultivated as far back as prehistoric times, and they have been found in Peruvian tombs dating back to 1500 BC. The Portuguese transported peanuts first to Africa, then to

Sesame seeds

Pistachio nuts

Sheer berenj | Persian rice pudding with cardamom

At its height the vast Persian empire spread from Baghdad and eastern Iraq, over the whole of Iran, through Afghanistan and parts of Pakistan to the east and in the other direction as far as the eastern half of modern-day Turkey. The empire's exquisite food, sumptuous with fruits, nuts, and spices, is still revered today.

Serves 4–6

1 cup short-grain rice

4 cups (1 quart) milk

1 scant cup superfine sugar

1 tablespoon honey

½ teaspoon ground cardamom

1 egg yolk

¼ cup heavy cream

2 tablespoons skinned pistachio nuts, coarsely chopped

1 Put the rice in a saucepan, and cover with cold water. Bring to the boil and simmer, uncovered, for 4 minutes. Drain the rice and return to the pan with the milk, sugar, and honey. Add the cardamom. Bring to the boil, then simmer over a low heat for 15 minutes, stirring regularly to avoid sticking, until the milk is absorbed.

2 Beat the egg yolk with the cream until pale, thick, and mousse-like. Add the pistachios, reserving some for garnish. When the rice is cooked, stir the cream mixture into the rice pudding. Serve hot, warm, or cold as is, or with poached or roasted fruits such as quince (see below), apricots, or rhubarb.

Compote e behi (Afghan caramelized quince compote) Quinces develop a rose-pink tinge and unique scent when cooked. If not available, use pears, apricots, or peaches. Using a mortar and pestle, crush 2 green cardamom pods and 4 cloves until fine. Pass through a fine sieve to remove any woody bits. Peel, quarter, and core 4 quinces, then put in a pan. Mix the sieved spices with ½ cup sugar, and scatter over the fruit. Add ⅔ cup water, and bring to the boil over a medium-high heat. Reduce the heat, and simmer for 50 minutes until the quinces are soft. Remove the fruit from the syrup with a slotted spoon. Simmer the liquid for about 5 minutes until reduced by half. Add the juice of ½ lemon and taste. If necessary, add a little extra sugar. Heat the broiler until hot. Place the poached quince quarters on a baking sheet lined with aluminum foil, and spoon over the scented syrup. Place under the broiler for 3–4 minutes until the tops are caramelized. Serve in bowls with the extra syrup, and heavy cream, crème fraîche, or ice cream, if desired. This compote works well with Yogurt and Pistachio Cake (pp186–7). Serves 4–6.

Partner with
Keralan spiced chickpea and lentil dumplings (pp56–7)
Lemon and saffron chicken kebabs (pp172–2)

Miwa naurozee | Afghan new year compote

Miwa means "fruit" and *nauroz* means the "new year," reflecting the roots of this compote of dried fruit and nuts that is traditionally prepared to celebrate the advent of spring, which is considered the new year in Afghanistan. It can be made with any combination of fruits or nuts, and served with cream or cream-based desserts.

1 Wash the apricots, raisins, and cherries, then put in a large bowl and cover with cold water. Let the fruits to soak for 2 days to ensure maximum plumpness.

2 Put the walnuts, almonds, and pistachios in a separate bowl, and cover with boiling water. Let the nuts soak until the water has cooled. Drain, then rub the skins from the nuts with a kitchen towel. Removing the skins from walnuts is time consuming, and you will need a small knife to get under the skins, but it is worth the effort. Set the nuts aside.

3 When the fruits have been soaked for 2 days, drain the liquid into a small pan. Add the honey, orange juice, cinnamon, nutmeg, allspice, and cloves. Bring to the boil, and simmer until the juices start to turn syrupy. Combine the fruits and nuts, then mix in the spiced syrup. Serve warm or chilled.

Serves 6

½ cup dried apricots

⅓ cup golden raisins

⅔ cup dark seedless raisins

⅓ cup dried sour cherries

⅓ cup walnuts

⅓ cup almonds

⅓ cup shelled pistachio nuts

2 tablespoons honey

juice of 1 orange

1 cinnamon stick

½ teaspoon freshly grated nutmeg

½ teaspoon ground allspice

½ teaspoon ground cloves

Partner with
Turkish zucchini fritters (p64)
Lamb pilaf with saffron and nuts (p104)

Sharbat | Sour cherry sherbet

A *sharbat*, or sherbet, is a refreshing fruit syrup cordial. On a hot day, pour it over crushed ice or dilute with mineral water for a thirst-quenching drink. You can also mix the base with some yogurt or cream, or pour it over ice cream or fresh fruit. Vary the fruits used to make the sherbet, from dried or semi-dried fruit, to strawberries and other berries, or ripe stone fruit.

Serves 6
⅔ cup dried sour cherries
⅓ cup dried cranberries
⅓ cup chopped dried figs
grated zest and juice of 1 orange
1 cinnamon stick
3 bay leaves
2 tablespoons honey
pinch of salt

1 Put the dried cherries, cranberries, and figs in a large bowl with the orange juice and zest, cinnamon, bay leaves, and honey. Add 2 cups boiling water. Cover and leave to stand for 40 minutes or until the fruit has absorbed as much of the liquid as possible.

2 Remove the fruit with a slotted spoon to another bowl. Pour the liquid into a small pan, add a pinch of salt, and simmer over medium heat for 6–7 minutes until the liquid has reduced by half and has started to become syrupy.

3 Pour the syrup back over the fruit and use immediately. Another suggestions is to use the fruit for one dish, maybe a dessert, and save the syrup to make a refreshing sherbet drink.

Tamarind sharbat Tamarind is used here to make a refreshing *sharbat* syrup, or cordial. Put a rough cake of 1lb (450g) pressed tamarind meat in a large bowl. Cover with 4 cups (1 quart) hot water. Leave to soften overnight, then massage the flesh away from the pits and stringy membranes. Rub the pulp through a fine sieve, squashing it with a wooden spoon. Sieve the pulp again, back into the soaking liquid. Strain through a clean muslin cloth into a pan. Add 1¾ cups sugar. Bring to the boil, stirring slowly to dissolve the sugar. Simmer gently until the syrup thickens. Allow to cool, then pour into clean, dry bottles and seal tightly. The high sugar content means that the syrup will keep stored in the refrigerator. (Increase the amount of sugar if the syrup is too sour for your taste.) Add a splash to a glass of chilled sparkling or still water to make a cooling drink.

Partner with
Grilled beef patties with shallots and cumin (pp26–7)
Sumatran minced duck sate (pp50–1)

Pineapple with caramelized chile

The heat of chiles counters the sweetness of the pineapple in this unusual combination. This dish goes one step further by caramelizing the sugar and dried chile, imparting a smoky flavor to this simple dish without cooking the pineapple. You can use this method for other fruits as well.

1 Peel the pineapple and cut in half lengthways. Cut each half into half-moon slices. Using a mortar and pestle, crush the sugar and dried chile until there are small fragments of sugar and crushed chile. Do not crush the sugar to dust.

2 Scatter the chile sugar over the pineapple, then light a chef's blowtorch (if you do not have one, preheat the broiler until very hot). Caramelize the sugar so that it smokes and blackens in parts. Repeat on all the slices, moving the flame around the fruit evenly and not leaving it in one area for too long—otherwise the sugar will be too bitter. Allow to cool slightly, and serve immediately.

Watermelon with lime, salt, and pepper In Thailand and Vietnam, small nuggets of tamarind meat are rolled in granulated sugar, then sprinkled with a little salt and dried chile. This dessert has the same effect, but with slightly subtler flavors. The combination can also be used to make a refreshing drink. Using a sharp knife, cut the top and the bottom off 1 small watermelon. Remove the skin, cutting from top to bottom, so that all the skin and the white areas of flesh have been cut away. Cut each half into wedges. If you view the melon wedge from side on, it is made up of three layers. The inside, or core, layer is smooth with no seeds. Remove this layer with a knife, and cut the flesh into bite-size chunks. Next, remove the second layer of seeds entirely. Cut the last, seed-free layer into bite-size chunks. Chill the diced watermelon for at least 1 hour. When ready to serve, juice 2 fresh limes and add to the melon. Season well with plenty of freshly ground black pepper and a good seasoning of salt. Do not be shy with these two flavorings. Mix together and taste—you will be pleasantly surprised. Serves 4–6.

Serves 4–6

1 fresh pineapple

3½oz (100g) yellow rock sugar (available from Chinese markets) or ½ cup Demerara sugar

½ teaspoon dried red chile flakes

Partner with
Marinated grilled mackerel (pp22–3)
Spiced shrimp cakes on sticks of lemongrass (pp34–5)

Goash-e-feel | Elephant ear pastries

You can make these pastries large or small. The name comes from the shape the pastries form when they are fried. There are many variations of how the are finished. They can be drizzled with a scented syrup made with orange flower water or rose water, or dusted with sugar and spices, or sprinkled with confectioners' sugar and ground pistachio nuts. *Goash-e-feel* are made all across once what was the vast Persian empire, so they may be found in Iran, Pakistan, Turkey, and Afghanistan.

Makes 16 small ones or 8 large

1 egg

1 tablespoon unsalted butter, melted

½ cup milk

2 cups all-purpose flour

pinch of salt

1 teaspoon confectioners' sugar

vegetable oil for shallow-frying

For the topping

¼ cup shelled pistachio nuts

¼ cup confectioners' sugar

2 teaspoons ground cinnamon

Partner with
Potato and cauliflower pakoras (pp66–7)
Gujarati eggplant fritters (pp82–3)

1 Beat the egg in a measuring cup and add the melted butter. Add just enough milk to fill the measuring cup to the ½-cup mark (4fl oz). In a bowl, sift the flour with a pinch of salt and a teaspoon of confectioners' sugar. Add the egg-milk mixture to the flour, and stir to form a dough. Turn the dough onto a lightly floured surface and knead for 8–10 minutes until smooth and elastic. Divide the dough in 16 pieces and shape in small balls. Place the balls on a lightly floured baking sheet, and let rest under a damp cloth for about 40 minutes.

2 On a lightly floured work surface, roll out each ball with a rolling pin into a circle that is as thin and as wide as possible. Using your fingers and thumb, pleat one half of each pastry disc, then nip together with dampened fingers so that the pleat holds together while the pastries are frying. To make the topping, grind the pistachio nuts until fine; mix the confectioners' sugar and cinnamon together. Have ready for when the pastries come out of the hot oil.

3 In a large frying pan, heat enough oil to shallow-fry the pastries over a medium-high heat. When the oil is hot, carefully put in the pastries one or two at a time, depending on the size of the pan. Fry for 1½–2 minutes on each side until golden. Remove the ears from the pan with a slotted spoon, carefully shaking off any excess oil. Drain on paper towels.

4 Allow the pastries to cool a little, then sprinkle first with the confectioners' sugar mixture, then the ground pistachio nuts. Serve warm or cold.

Pomegranate and blood orange fruit salad

During the winter, one of the highlights of what can otherwise seem a bleak time of the year is the bounty of citrus fruits. In this brightly colored winter fruit salad, blood oranges and pomegranates are spiked with Eastern spices. Like many fruit dishes from Central Asia, it tastes indulgent, exotic, and refreshing.

Serves 4–6

4 blood oranges or juicy navel oranges

4 mandarin oranges

2 pomegranates

1 teaspoon runny honey

2 green cardamom pods

1 teaspoon ground cinnamon or 1 cinnamon stick

⅔ cup skinned pistachio nuts, coarsely chopped

Partner with
Minced pork balls with garlic and pepper (pp38–9)
Sichuan chicken dumplings (p100)

1 With a knife, remove the peel and pith from the blood and mandarin oranges. Over a small non-corrosive saucepan, segment an orange using the knife, by cutting just inside the dividing membrane of the segments. Save any juice in the pan. When all the segments are divided, squeeze the remaining pith and membrane to extract all the juice possible. Repeat with all the fruit. Put the orange segments in a bowl and set aside.

2 To seed the pomegranate, take the whole fruit in your hand and, using a wooden spoon, tap it firmly all over about 20 times. This loosens the seeds inside so that they can be removed. Cut the fruit in half with a knife (there will be a lot of juice to add to the pan of orange juice). Over a bowl, again tap the halved fruit on the skin with a wooden spoon, so that all the seeds fall out and the bitter white pith is left behind.

3 Add the honey to the pan of juices. With the back of a knife or a wooden spoon, crush the cardamom pods to release the central seeds that contain the oils. Discard the husks, and add the seeds to the pan. Sprinkle in the ground cinnamon (a whole cinnamon stick can be used instead of the powder), and stir to incorporate all the ingredients. Bring the citrus juices and spices to the boil, and simmer for 1 minute. Remove from the heat and set the liquid aside to allow to cool and for the flavors to infuse.

4 When cool, pour over the segmented citrus fruit. Mix together with the pomegranate seeds. Chill until needed. To serve, scatter the pistachio nuts over the marinated fruit, and serve as a light and colorful end to a meal or with Greek-style yogurt, crème fraîche, or ice cream, or to moisten a Mediterranean orange cake.

Pear fritters with cinnamon honey syrup

Alter the aromatic element of the syrup by using various herbs or dried spices or by adding vanilla or ginger. A few sprigs of rosemary could also be used – this syrup can be paired with apples, pears, or quince.

1 To make the cinnamon honey syrup, combine the honey and wine in a pan. Simmer for 3–4 minutes with the cinnamon sticks until slightly reduced, then leave to cool.

2 Next make the batter. Whisk together the egg yolks, wine, milk, and olive oil, then slowly add the flour, whisking all the time until the batter is smooth. Beat the egg whites in a clean bowl with an electric mixer until they form soft peaks. Stir one-third of the egg whites into the flour mixture to loosen, then gently fold in the remaining egg whites.

3 Heat the oil in a deep saucepan until hot but not smoking – a splash of batter should sizzle immediately. Peel, halve, and core the pears, then cut each pear half into six slices lengthways.

4 Dip the pear slices into the batter, allowing any excess to drain off. Deep-fry the pear slices for 4 minutes or until golden and puffed, turning once during the cooking time. Cook in batches, to keep the temperature of the oil from dropping too much and ensure that your fritters are crisp. Drain on paper towels, and keep warm in the oven while cooking the remaining fritters. Repeat the process until all the pear slices have been used. Serve immediately with the cinnamon honey syrup drizzled over the fritters.

Serves 6

light vegetable oil for deep-frying

4 ripe pears

For the cinnamon honey syrup

3 tablespoons honey

¼ cup sweet wine such as Vin Santo or Muscat*

2 cinnamon sticks

For the batter

2 eggs, separated

½ cup sweet white wine*

½ cup milk

2 tablespoons extra virgin olive oil

1 cup all-purpose flour

* If sweet wine is not available, use white wine with 1½ tablespoons superfine sugar.

Partner with
Chinese barbecue spare ribs (pp24–5)
Pork and cabbage dumplings (p75)

Kaymakli kurk kayisi | Stuffed apricots

Apricots were orginally native to China, but their gradual spread through trade means that they are now found across Asia, as well as other parts of the world. These stuffed apricots make a moreish snack, particularly served with coffee, and work well as part of a larger dessert selection. Figs or dates can also be used for this dish. This dessert is simple to make, but very impressive. Always buy the plumpest dried fruits available, rather than ones that are old and shriveled.

Serves 6

1lb (450g) dried apricots or dates

1 scant cup sugar

3 green cardamom pods

1 cinnamon stick

2 cloves

juice of ½ lemon

3 tablespoons mascarpone or heavy cream

¼ cup skinned pistachio nuts, finely ground

1 Put the dried fruit in a bowl, cover with water, and soak overnight until they are swollen and softened. The next day, remove the apricots from the liquid to a bowl using a slotted spoon. Add enough water to the soaking liquid so there are 2½ cups (600ml) of liquid.

2 Pour the liquid into a pan, and add the sugar, cardamom, cinnamon, and cloves. Slowly bring to the boil to dissolve the sugar. Simmer for 10 minutes, then add the soaked apricots. Simmer the apricots for another 10 minutes until they have softened further and the liquid has become syrupy. Add the lemon juice and cook for another minute. Remove from the heat, and take out the apricots using a slotted spoon. Allow both the apricots and the syrup to cool.

3 Mix the mascarpone or cream with 3 tablespoons of the cooled apricot syrup. When the apricots have cooled, split them in half and fill with the mascarpone mxiture. Sprinkle the ground pistachio nuts over the top, and serve.

Partner with
Lamb pilaf with saffron
and nuts (p104)
Spiced stuffed eggplant (p165)
Elephant ear pastries (pp196-7)

Keynotes | **Aromatic spices**

The potent alchemy of spices of the East conjure up images of ancient trade routes, riches, intrigue, and mystery. Wars have been waged and conquests made over these bounteous aromatics. Spices were

These spices were Asia's best and most valuable export long before people in the West knew what the people of these lands looked like or what other foods they ate.

Asia's best and most valuable export long before people in the West knew what the people of these lands looked like or what other foods they ate.

Spices became popular for their flavor and the sense of grandeur they gave to food. They were also widely used in pickling and preserving, and to mask the intense flavor of putrid and spoiled food. At one time, salt for preserving was expensive; cold weather was the only other main food preservation method. In Elizabethan times, spices were more widely used in a kitchen than today for this reason. For some, the aromas of these spices often create an image of Christmas and other holidays. Cured hams are often studded with cloves. Fruit pies including apple and pumpkin, gingerbread cakes and figures, and festive cookies all contain spices once considered rare and precious.

Another important factor in the use of spices in preserving is the antiseptic qualities found in a number of them. The oils in cinnamon, cloves, ginger, white mustard seeds, aniseed, juniper, and pepper are all powerful preservatives.

Cinnamon

Cinnamon (*Cinnamomum verum*) has a distinctive smell that is warm, sweet, and comforting. The cinnamon sticks, or quills, come from the inner bark of an evergreen camphor laurel that is related to the bay tree. Originally native to Sri Lanka, but now grown in China and all over Asia, as well as on the Caribbean spice island of Grenada, cinnamon is widely used in the cuisines of India, Vietnam, Morocco, Iran, and Malaysia, in both savory and sweet dishes. The powdered form, though convenient, is inferior to the cinnamon sticks because it goes stale and loses its flavor. The best way to use any spice is whole; if you need ground spice, grind it yourself.

Star anise

Star anise (*Illicium verum*) is a star-shaped seed pod; its intrigue lies in its beauty and also its incredibly intense taste. It has much more robust aniseed and licorice-like flavors than regular anise seeds, and works well with braises and slow-cooked dishes. Star anise, one of the main ingredients of Chinese five-spice powder, often scents the very air that you breathe in any Chinatown or Chinese community around the world. In Europe, the popularity of this jewel of a spice dates back to the 16th century. The famous Vietnamese soup called *pho*, a name which comes from the French *pot-au-feu* (pot on the fire), has an intense stock perfumed with star anise, cinnamon, and ginger.

Cassia

Although cassia (*Cinnamomum burmannii*) is similar to cinnamon and has a similar fragrance, the two should not be confused. Cassia is the bark of a related tree native to the northeast Indian state of Assam and to Burma; the part used as a spice is the outer bark. It has a much more robust and pronounced aroma than cinnamon. Preferred in Indian, Burmese, Vietnamese, and Chinese cuisines, its toughness makes it harder to grind, so either leave whole or use some that has already been ground.

Clove

The English name for this small, highly aromatic spice is derived from the Latin word *clavus*, which means "nail". In India, cloves are sometimes used for exactly that – to fasten small paper packets. The dried unopened flower buds of

Cloves

Cinnamon quills

Star anise

Cardamom pods

a tree that comes from the myrtle family (*Syzygium aromaticum*), cloves have a very powerful flavor and should be used sparingly; their pungent taste creates a numbing sensation, which is why they are used the world over for toothache. Used in sweet and savory dishes, cloves appear in spice mixes such as Chinese five-spice and are used for pickling and preserving, and for their antiseptic properties. They are commonly found in Middle Eastern sweet pastries.

Nutmeg

The common or fragrant nutmeg tree (*Myristica fragrans*) is indigenous to the Moluccas, and yields two different spices from the same fruit: nutmeg and mace. A warm, sweet spice, nutmeg should not be overused for two reasons: it has a strong flavor and is a potent hallucinogen. In India, nutmeg is used almost exclusively in sweet dishes and sometimes in garam masala. In the Middle East, nutmeg is often used for savory dishes, while Japanese varieties of curry powder include nutmeg.

Mangosteen, lychee, and mango salad

Mangosteens are a fruit with a dark, hard skin that gives nothing away of the sumptuous flesh that is inside. The flesh is white and has the extraordinary taste of a combination of wild strawberries, bananas, and citrus. They are available in Hawaii, Puerto Rico, and Canada, but almost impossible to find in the continental United States. If unavailable, use other tropical fruits, such as pineapple and papaya.

Serves 4–6

4 kaffir lime leaves

18 lychees

2 ripe mangoes

8 mangosteens

20 fresh mint leaves

For the passion fruit dressing

1¾in (4cm) piece of fresh ginger, finely chopped

1 tablespoon superfine sugar

2 passion fruits

juice of 1 orange

juice of 1 lime

Partner with
Stir-fried beef with chile and onion relish (p33)
Pickled daikon salad with fried garlic (p142)

1 Using a knife, shave off the raised stem on the back of the kaffir lime leaves so that the leaves are flat. Tightly roll the leaves into a cigar shape. Working the knife rhythmically, finely shred the rolled lime leaves into thin slivers. Set aside.

2 With the skin still on the lychees, cut each one in half through the pit, then slip off the skins and discard the stones. Peel the mango and cut the flesh into large lobes, then cut into equal-sized slices about ½in (1cm) thick. To open the mangosteens, make a horizontal cut around the middle of the fruit with a small serrated knife. Cut until the half lifts off. Be careful, as the skin is very hard, so you will have to press quite firmly. The outer pith of the fruit is red and the fruit is white. Remove and discard the hard black pits inside.

3 To make the passion fruit dressing, use a mortar and pestle to crush the ginger with the sugar, to form a smooth paste. Halve the passion fruits, and scrape the pulp into the ginger paste. Stir, then mix with the orange and lime juice.

4 Gently mix the lychee, mango, and mangosteen in a large bowl. Sprinkle with the mint leaves and shredded lime leaves, and stir through carefully. Add the dressing and gently stir through again. Serve immediately as a refreshing end to any meal.

Doogh | Yogurt and mint drink

Many variations of this very refreshing drink with ancient origins are found across Asia, from what was the Persian empire through to the Indian subcontinent. Some variations are sweet, while others are more salty and sour. What they all have in common is that they pick you up when are faced with too much heat. *Doogh* is a truly thirst-quenching drink with a long-lasting effect. It can be made with plain or sparkling water, served chilled from the refrigerator, or poured over ice cubes or crushed ice.

1 Whisk the yogurt and sour cream together in a large pitcher with the lemon juice and salt until smoothly blended. Add the cucumber and mint, and stir through.

2 Stir in 4 cups (1 quart) water—plain or sparkling—and mix together so that it does not separate. Keep in the refrigerator, ready to use, until you need this thirst-quencher. The combination of salt and acidity is just what's needed to revive you on a hot day.

Serves 4–6

1 lb (450g) Greek-style yogurt

¼ cup sour cream

juice of 1 lemon

1 tablespoon salt

1 small Persian cucumber, peeled and grated

3 sprigs of fresh mint, leaves picked and coarsely chopped

Partner with
Burmese turmeric
fishcakes (p80)
Potato with turmeric and
mustard seeds (pp174–5)

Bastani sa labi | Saffron ice cream with pistachio nuts

Persian ice cream is perfumed with rose water, saffron, and pistachio nuts. There is also an interesting textural note to Persian ice cream. Just before the end of the freezing process, small chips of frozen heavy cream are stirred into the ice cream. When the ice cream is eaten, these chewy pieces provide a contrast to the creamy texture of the rest of the tempting dessert.

Serves 4

4 cups (1 quart) milk

1¼ cups superfine sugar

3 tablespoons Greek-style yogurt

2 teaspoons rose water

1 teaspoon saffron threads, soaked in 2 tablespoons boiling milk

2 tablespoons frozen chips heavy cream, to be added at the end of freezing

3 tablespoons chopped pistachio nuts

1 Bring the milk to the boil over a medium-high heat, then remove the pan from the heat. Beat together the yogurt and sugar in a bowl until all the sugar has dissolved. Whisk in the milk, then add the rose water and the saffron and its liquid.

2 Pour into the ice-cream machine, and freeze and churn for 30 minutes according to the manufacturer's instructions. (If you do not have an ice-cream maker, then pour the mixture in a pan. Every 10 minutes, remove the ice cream from the freezer and whisk for a couple of minutes, then return to the freezer once more.)

3 Five minutes before the end of the freezing process, remove the frozen heavy cream from the freezer, and chop into small nuggets. Add the nuggets to the churning ice cream, if using an ice-cream machine, or stir through the ice cream just before it becomes softly firm if making in a pan. When the ice cream is softly firm, scoop into a plastic container and keep covered in the freezer until needed.

4 To serve, garnish the golden ice cream with the pistachio nuts. Serve as an accompaniment to roasted fruits or cakes such as the Yogurt and Pistachio Cake on pp186–7.

Partner with
Afghan caramelized quince compote (p190)
Afghan new year compote (p191)

Menu ideas

Part of the pleasure of experiencing food from other parts of the world is learning to mix and match flavors and food styles. The following menus are designed to start you on your way, so that you can embark on a tasting journey through the various cuisines with friends and family. They are a guide only, so feel free to experiment. Sampling different taste sensations in a single meal is an excellent way to whet your appetite for more. An added bonus is that these recipes all work well for entertaining — impress your guests with your culinary repertoire.

Menu 1

◁ Stir-fried greens with garlic **Vietnam** pp18–19

Chinese barbecue spare ribs **China** pp24–5

Tamarind fried shrimp **Malaysia** pp154–5

Scallion and chive flower rolls **China** pp110–11

Grilled eggplant salad **Burma** pp128–9

Menu 2

◁ Marinated grilled mackerel **Indonesia** pp22–3

Pork and cabbage dumplings **Korea** p75

Crisp cabbage salad with peanuts **Laos** pp134–5

Fresh coconut chutney **Singapore** p133

Crisp peanut wafers **Indonesia** p65

Watermelon with lime, salt, and pepper **Modern Asian** p195

Menu 3

◁ Steamed shrimp wontons **China** pp98–9

Seared scallops with fresh chutney **India** pp16–17

Grilled beef patties with shallots and cumin **Vietnam** pp26–7

Scallion pancakes **Korea** pp60–1

Nonya bean curd salad **Singapore** pp136–7

Menu 4

◁ Burmese spiced split pea fritters **Burma** pp90–1

Isaan-style grilled chicken **Thailand** pp40–1

Spiced shrimp cakes on sticks of lemongrass **Vietnam** pp34–5

Fried bean sprouts and clams **Malaysia** pp94–5

Potato with turmeric and mustard seeds **Singapore** pp174–5

Menu 5

◁ Sesame chicken salad with white pepper **China** pp118–19

Nonya-style spicy pork **Singapore** pp114–5

Curried sweet corn fritters **Thailand** pp70–1

Carrot pachadi **India** pp162–3

Garlic and cilantro naan **India** p49

Pear fritters with cinnamon honey syrup **Iran** pp202–3

Menu 6

◁ Marinated barbecue beef **Korea** pp52–3

North Vietnamese fish brochettes **Vietnam** pp46–7

Korean hot pickled cabbage **Korea** p164

Mushroom pot-stickers **China** pp106–7

Tomato chutney with green chile **India** p179

Menu 7

◁ Keralan spiced chickpea and lentil dumplings **India** pp56–7

Miso soup with seven-spice chicken **Japan** pp96–7

Indonesian fried rice **Indonesia** p32

Stir-fried beef with chile and onion relish **Thailand** p33

Pickled daikon salad with fried garlic **Burma** p142

Menu 8

◁ Potato and cauliflower pakoras **Afghanistan** pp 66–7

Sardines with green chile sambal **Malaysia** pp44–5

Sichuan chicken dumplings **China** p100

Cured shrimp with shredded lime leaves **Thailand** p123

Mangosteen, lychee, and mango salad **Modern Asian** pp208

Menu 9

◁ Gujarati eggplant fritters **India** pp82–3

Sumatran duck sate **Indonesia** pp50–1

Sesame tempura **Japan** pp78–9

Sichuan peppered beef **China** pp170–1

Stir-fried bean sprouts with chile bean paste **Korea** p21

Menu 10

◁ Malay beef rendang **Malaysia** pp148–9

Pork balls with garlic and pepper **Vietnam** pp38–9

Steamed green vegetable rolls **Korea** p106

Sri Lankan smoky eggplant dip **Sri Lanka** pp151–2

Rice flour pancakes **Sri Lanka** p81

Citrus and young coconut jelly **Thailand** pp00–00

Menu 11

◁ Hot and sour green papaya salad **Thailand** pp118–19

Tamarind beef with peanuts **Vietnam** pp180–1

Malaysian fried noodles **Malaysia** p20

Shrimp and chive spring rolls **China** pp72–3

Chilled seared tuna with ginger **Japan** pp120–1

Menu 12

◁ Pineapple with caramelized chile **Modern Asian** pp194–5

Fresh lettuce cups with chicken **China** pp124–5

Singapore coconut laksa **Singapore** p112

Roast pork with fresh mint and peanuts **Vietnam** pp158–9

Laotian spice-pickled spring onions **Laos** pp168–9

Menu 13

◁ Asian salad with pea shoots and sprouts **Modern Asian** pp140–1

Spicy lamb-stuffed pancakes **Singapore** p74

Happy crêpes **Vietnam** pp86–7

Sashimi of sea bass with hot dressing **Korea** p143

Sumatran eggplant sambal **Indonesia** pp88–9

Menu 14

◁ Spicy apricot chutney **Afghanistan** pp160–1

Lamb pilaf with saffron and nuts **Pakistan** p104

Spiced stuffed eggplant **Turkey** p165

Fried puffed potato bread **India** pp62–3

Afghan new year compote **Afghanistan** p191

Menu 15

◁ Fried squid flowers with ginger and spices **China** pp58–9

Burmese turmeric fishcakes **Burma** p80

Steamed barbecue pork buns **China** p101

Spicy green beans with chile **Singapore** pp30–1

Fried eggplant with toasted sesame seeds **Korea** p178

Menu 16

◁ Chilled soba noodles with seared salmon **Japan** pp130–1

Nonya pork, shrimp, and crab ball soup **Malaysia** p113

Lemon and saffron chicken kebabs **Iran** pp172–3

Scallion and chive flower rolls **China** pp110–11

Pomegranate and blood orange fruit salad **Iran** pp200–1

Glossary

agar agar A natural gelling agent used in Asia (sometimes known as *kanten*), agar agar is derived from seaweed; it comes in blocks, as a powder, or in strands, and can be found in Thai and other Asian markets and health food shops. If unavailable, substitute with gelatine leaves or powdered gelatine (agar agar sets more easily, so you may need to adjust amounts).

asafoetida powder Ground from a plant that is similar to fennel, asafoetida powder has an extremely pungent garlic-like smell and should be used sparingly. Found mostly in Indian cooking, it is a flavor enhancer. It can be found in Indian markets.

bok choy Part of the Brassica family, bok choy is also known as Chinese white cabbage and white mustard cabbage. It is used in salad and stir-fries.

Chinese cabbage Also called napa cabbage, celery cabbage, and Peking cabbage, Chinese cabbage is part of the mustard family. Not to be confused with bok choy, it is used in salads and stir-fries.

choi sum Another member of the cabbage family, this is also called flowering white cabbage and Chinese flowering cabbage. Choi sum is used in salads and stir-fries, and is available from Asian and Chinese markets, and farmers' and produce markets.

daikon Also known as mooli, Japanese radish, Chinese radish, or Oriental radish, this long root vegetable has crisp white flesh; the skin is either creamy white or black. Look for daikon with unwrinkled skin. Daikon can be used raw in salads or as a garnish, or cooked in stir-fries. It is available from Japanese, Indian, and Asian markets.

dashi Dashi is a Japanese stock made with *katsuobushi* (dried bonito flakes) and *kombu* (dried kelp seaweed).

fish sauce This pungent liquid made from fermented anchovies or other fish is an essential Southeast Asian ingredient. Its loses its fishiness on cooking, mellowing to add flavor. Recipes for this vary, but can be used interchangeably. Known as *nam pla* in Thailand and *nuoc nam* in Vietnam, it is available in supermarkets and Asian markets.

galangal Especially popular in Thai cuisine, galangal (see p29) is a hot and peppery aromatic rhizome. A little like ginger, it is used as a seasoning throughout Southeast Asia and South India. It is available both fresh and dried from Asian markets.

ketjap manis Favored in Indonesia, ketjap (or kecap) manis is similar to soy sauce, but is sweetened with palm sugar. It contains seasonings such as star anise and garlic. It can be found at Southeast Asian markets and Chinese supermarkets.

kochujang Also known as kochu chang, this is a fiery red paste from Korea made from fermented soy or black beans and red chiles. Sunchang kochujang comes from the region of the same name, where it is a speciality. It is available from Korean and other Asian markets.

kombu Commonly used in Japanese cooking, kombu is kelp seaweed that has been dried in the sun before being folded into sheets. Kombu is used in combination with dried bonito flakes for the Japanese stock *dashi*, as well as for sushi and other dishes. The sun-dried kelp acts as a flavor enhancer. It was from kelp that the Japanese first extracted monosodium glutamate (MSG). Kombu is available from supermarkets and Japanese and Asian markets, and some health foodo shops.

palm sugar Made from the sap of date or coconut palms, this is also known as coconut sugar, gur, and jaggery. In India, the term *jaggery* also refers to sugar refined from raw sugar cane. Look for it in Asian markets.

rock sugar A type of Chinese sugar, rock sugar is crystallized in large chunks, which then need to be broken up for use in cooking. It is not as sweet as ordinary granulated sugar and can be found at Asian markets and Chinese supermarkets.

sambal oelek A sambal is a spicy and fiery paste made from primarily from chiles, which is served as a condiment. Sambal oelek is perhaps the most basic type, made with chiles, brown sugar, and salt. It is available in jars from Asian markets.

Shaoxing rice wine Rice wine is made by fermenting glutinous rice or millet. In China, Shaoxing rice wine, from the province of Zheijang, is considered to be the finest. Make sure that you buy true rice wine from a Chinese supermarket or Asian market; if unavailable, substitute with a good-quality dry sherry.

shichimi togarashi Also known as Japanese seven-spice, shichimi togarashi (see p69) is available from Japanese and Asian grocers. It can be sprinkled over udon noodles or on fish or meat before cooking.

shrimp paste This is made from salted fermented prawns, and recipes vary slightly depending on where it is made. It should be used only sparingly and is available from Asian markets.

sour cherry The sour cherry (*Prunus cerasus*) is smaller than its sweet counterpart; there are several varieties, including Aleppo, Montmorency, and Morello. Fresh sour (tart) cherries are usually available from late spring to early summer. The Montmorency is overwhelmingly the most popular US-grown sour variety. Dried sour cherries are a perfect substitute and can be found at supermarkets.

tamarind An essential ingredient in Indian and Southeast Asian cooking, tamarind is also found in Middle Eastern and Persian recipes. The fruit of the tamarind are large pods yielding both seeds and a tart pulp. Used as a flavoring in much the same way as lemon juice, the pulp comes in concentrated form in jars, as a paste, in a dried brick, or as a powder. It is available from Indian, Asian, and some Middle Eastern markets.

Thai basil See p139. If Thai basil is not available, substitute a combination of fresh cilantro and mint leaves.

Vietnamese mint See p139.

young coconut Young (green) coconut is available shredded and frozen in its sweet water from Chinese, Thai, other Asian, and Indian markets. It is also available in cans, but the frozen alternative is better.

Useful websites

India and Sri Lanka
www.kalustyans.com
www.kamdarplaza.com
www.zamourispices.com

Japan and Korea
www.uwajimaya.com
www.fujiya.ca
www.koamart.com

China and Southeast Asia
www.uwajimaya.com
www.templeofthai.com
www.importfood.com
www.pacificrimgourmet.com

Central and Western Asia
www.kalustyans.com
www.daynasmarket.com
www.tasteofturkey.com

General
www.kalustyans.com
www.penzeys.com
www.asianfoodgrocer.com
www.ethnicgrocer.com

Index

A

Afghan new year compote 191
aloo chaat 174
aloo puri 62
appam 81
apricots: Afghan new year
    compote 191
    spicy apricot chutney 160
    stuffed apricots 204
asam udang 154
Asian salad with pea shoots
    and sprouts 140

B

bakwan kepiting 113
ban khoai 86
basil 139
bastani sa labi 210
bean curd 43
    Nonya bean curd salad 137
bean sprouts: Asian salad with pea
    shoots and 140
    fried clams and 94
    happy crêpes 86
    roast pork with fresh mint and
      peanuts 159
    stir-fried bean sprouts with chile
      bean paste 21
beef: grilled beef patties 26
    Malay beef rendang 148
    marinated barbecue beef 52
    Sichuan peppered beef 171
    stir-fried beef with chile and
      onion relish 33
    tamarind beef with peanuts 180
black vinegar dipping sauce 122
bread: fried puffed potato bread 62
    garlic and cilantro naan 49
brochettes *see* kebabs
bulgogi 52
bun bi suon 159
Burmese spiced split pea fritters 90
Burmese turmeric fishcakes 80

C

cabbage: crisp cabbage salad 134
    Korean hot pickled cabbage 164
    pork and cabbage dumplings 75
cake, yogurt and pistachio 187
caramelized quince compote 191
carrot *pachadi* 163
cashew nuts 188–9
cassia 207
cauliflower and potato pakoras 67
cha bo 26
cha ca nuong 46
chamandhi 133
chao tom 34
char siu 48
char siu bao 101
cheese: Turkish zucchini fritters 64
cherries: sour cherry sherbet 192
chicken: lemon and saffron chicken
    kebabs 172
    fresh lettuce cups with 124
    Isaan-style grilled chicken 41
    Malaysian fried noodles 20
    miso soup with seven-spice
      chicken 97
    sesame chicken salad 118
    Sichuan chicken dumplings 100
    Sumatran duck sate 51
chickpeas: Gujarati eggplant
    fritters 82
    Keralan spiced chickpea and
      lentil dumplings 56
chiles 84–5
    chile and onion relish 33
    hot and sour green papaya
      salad 144
    Isaan dipping sauce 41
    Malay beef rendang 148
    Malaysian fried noodles 20
    marinated grilled mackerel 22
    nuoc cham dipping sauce 26, 38
    pineapple with caramelized
      chile 195
    sardines with green chile
      sambal 45
    seared scallops with fresh
      chutney 16

spicy green beans with 30
Sumatran eggplant
    sambal 89
tomato chutney with green
    chile 179
Chinese barbecue pork 48
Chinese barbecue spare ribs 25
Chinese cabbage: steamed green
    vegetable rolls 105
cho go chu jang 143
chuan wei hun tun 100
chun juan 73
chutney 16
    fresh coconut 133
    spicy apricot 160
    tomato with green chile 179
chutni zardolu 160
cilantro 138–9
    fresh coconut chutney 133
    garlic and cilantro naan 49
cinnamon 206
citrus and young coconut
    jelly 184
citrus dipping sauce 122
citrus fruit 176–7
clams, fried bean sprouts
    and 94
cloves 207
coconut: fresh coconut
    chutney 133
    citrus and young coconut
      jelly 184
coconut cream: Malay beef
    rendang 148
    Singapore coconut laksa 112
compote a behi 191
crab: Nonya pork, shrimp, and crab
    ball soup 113
    sesame tempura 78
crêpes, happy 86
cucumber: Nonya bean curd
    salad 137
    roast pork with fresh mint and
      peanuts 159
    Sichuan spicy pickled 152
    yogurt and mint drink 209
curry leaves 69

D

daikon: pickled daikon salad 142
dashi stock 97
dipping sauces: black vinegar 122
  citrus 122
  ginger and sesame 61
  Isaan 41
  nuoc cham 26, 38
  Sri Lankan eggplant dip 151
  Vietnamese peanut 153
doogh 209
duck: Sumatran duck sate 51
dumplings: Keralan spiced chickpea
    and lentil 56
  mushroom pot-sticker 107
  pork and cabbage 75
  Sichuan chicken 100
  scallion and chive flower
    rolls 110

E

eggplants: grilled eggplant
    salad 128
  fried eggplant with toasted
    sesame seeds 178
  Gujarati eggplant fritters 82
  spiced stuffed eggplant 165
  Sri Lankan eggplant dip 151
  Sumatran eggplant sambal 89
elephant ear pastries 196

F

fermented bean products 43
fish: Burmese turmeric fishcakes 80
  Singapore coconut laksa 112
  North Vietnamese fish
    brochettes 46
  preserved fish products 156–7
fish sauce 157
fritters: Burmese spiced split pea 90
  curried sweet corn 70
  Gujarati eggplant 82
  pear with honey and
    cinnamon 203
  potato and cauliflower pakoras 67
  sesame tempura 78
  Turkish zucchini fritters 64

G

galangal 29
garam masala 68
garlic and cilantro naan 49
ginger 28–9
  fried squid flowers with 58
  ginger and sesame dipping
    sauce 61
  sesame and ginger vinaigrette 98
glutinous rice 103
goash-e-feel 196
goenmande 75
green beans with chile 30
greens, stir-fried with garlic 19
Grilled eggplant salad 128
Gujarati eggplant fritters 82

H

har gau 98
hei jiao niu rou 171
herbs 138–9
hua juan 110

I

ice cream with saffron 210
ikan panggang 22
imam bayildi 165
Indonesian fried rice 32
iri goma tempura 78
Isaan dipping sauce 41
Isaan-style grilled chicken 41

J

jelly, citrus and young coconut 184
jiaozi 107
joojeh kabab 172

K

kabak mücveri 64
kacang panjang 30
kaffir lime leaves 177
  cured shrimp with 123
kaffir limes 177
kai ge 178
kai yaang 41
katsuo tataki 121
kaymakli kurk kayisi 204

kebabs: chicken kebab 172
  North Vietnamese fish
    brochettes 46
Keralan spiced chickpea and lentil
    dumplings 56
khayanthee thoke 128
kimchee 164
kombu: citrus dipping sauce 122
Korean hot pickled cabbage 164
kung sang wa 123

L

laksa lemak 112
lamb: lamb pilaf with saffron and
    nuts 104
  spicy lamb-stuffed pancakes 74
Laotian spice-pickled
    scallions 168
lemon 177
  citrus and young coconut
    jelly 184
  citrus dipping sauce 122
lemongrass 177
lentils: Kerala spiced chickpea and
    lentil dumplings 56
lettuce cups with chicken 124
limes 177
  citrus dipping sauce 122
  hot and sour green papaya
    salad 144
  nuoc cham dipping sauce 26, 38
lychee, mangosteen, and mango
    salad 208

M

mackerel, marinated grilled 22
Malaysian fried noodles 20
manda uppilittathu 132
mandu 105
mango pickle, South Indian 132
mangosteen, lychee, and mango
    salad 208
marinated barbecue beef 52
mee goreng 20
mint 139
  yogurt and mint drink 209
miso 42

miso soup with seven-spice
   chicken 97
miso shiru 97
miwa naurozee 191
monlar oo thoke 142
murtabak 74
mushrooms: happy crêpes 86
   Indonesian fried rice 32
   pot-stickers 107
   steamed green vegetable
      rolls 105

N

naam jaew 41
naan 49
naan, garlic and cilantro 49
nam prik pow 33
nasi goreng 32
nem nuong 38
ngephe gyaw 80
Nonya pork, shrimp, and crab ball
   soup 113
Nonya bean curd salad 137
Nonya-style spicy pork 114
noodles 103
   chilled soba noodles with seared
      salmon 131
   Singapore coconut laksa 112
   Malaysian fried noodles 20
   shrimp and chive spring
      rolls 73
North Vietnamese fish
   brochettes 46
nuoc cham dipping sauce 26, 38
nuoc dau phung 153
nutmeg 207
nuts 188–9
   Afghan new year compote 191
   lamb pilaf with saffron and 104
   yogurt and pistachio cake 187

O

onions: chile and onion relish 33
oranges: citrus and young coconut
   jelly 184
   pomegranate and blood orange
      fruit salad 200

P

pa jeon 61
pachadi, carrot 163
paigu 25
pakoras, potato and cauliflower 67
pancakes: happy crêpes 86
   rice flour pancakes 81
   scallion pancakes 61
   spicy lamb-stuffed pancakes 74
papaya: hot and sour green papaya
   salad 144
pastries, elephant ear 196
patta kaah ju chatni 16
pe chan gyaw 90
pea shoots, Asian salad with
   sprouts and 140
peanuts 189
   crisp cabbage salad with 134
   crisp peanut wafers 65
   roast pork with fresh mint and
      peanuts 159
   tamarind beef with 180
   Vietnamese peanut dipping
      sauce 153
pear fritters 203
peas, split: Burmese spiced split
   pea fritters 90
Persian ice cream 210
Persian rice pudding 190
phat neua 33
pickles: Korean hot pickled
   cabbage 164
   Laotian spice-pickled
      scallions 168
   pickled daikon salad with fried
      garlic 142
   Sichuan spicy pickled
      cucumber 152
   South Indian mango pickle 132
pilaf, lamb 104
pineapple with caramelized
   chile 195
pistachio nuts 188
   yogurt and pistachio cake 187
pomegranate and blood orange fruit
   salad 200

ponzu 122
pork: Chinese barbecue pork 48
   Chinese barbecue spare ribs 25
   happy crêpes 86
   pork balls with garlic and
      pepper 38
   Nonya pork, shrimp, and crab
      ball soup 113
   Nonya-style spicy pork 114
   pork and cabbage dumplings 75
   roast pork with fresh mint and
      peanuts 159
   steamed barbecue pork
      buns 101
potatoes: fried puffed potato
      bread 62
   potato and cauliflower pakoras 67
   with turmeric and mustard
      seeds 174
shrimp: Burmese turmeric
      fishcakes 80
   cured shrimp with shredded lime
      leaves 123
   happy crêpes 86
   Malaysian fried noodles 20
   Nonya pork, shrimp, and crab
      ball soup 113
   shrimp and chive spring rolls 73
   sesame tempura 78
   Singapore coconut laksa 112
   spiced shrimp cakes on sticks of
      lemongrass 34
   steamed shrimp wontons 98
   tamarind fried shrimp 154
preserved fish products 156–7
puri, potato 62

Q

quince compote, caramelized 191

R

raisins: Afghan new year
   compote 191
rau xanh toi xao 19
relish, chile and onion 33
rempeyek kacang 65
rendang daging 148

rice 102–3
  glutinous rice 103
  Indonesian fried rice 32
  lamb pilaf 104
  Persian rice pudding 190
rice flour pancakes 81
rice noodles 103
rice paper wrappers 103
  shrimp and chive spring rolls 73
ringrah na bhajia 82

S
saffron, Persian ice cream
  with 210
salads: Asian salad with pea shoots
    and sprouts 140
  crisp cabbage salad 134
  grilled eggplant salad 128
  hot and sour green papaya
    salad 144
  Nonya bean curd salad 137
  pickled daikon salad 142
  roast pork with fresh mint and
    peanuts 159
  sesame chicken salad 118
salmon, chilled soba noodles
  with 131
sambals 85
  green chile 45
  Sumatran eggplant 89
sambal babi 114
sambal lado mudo 45
san choy bau 124
sardines with green chile sambal 45
sashimi of sea bass 143
sate lilit bebek 51
sauces *see* dipping sauces
scallops with fresh chutney 16
sea bass, sashimi of 143
seeds 188
sesame and ginger vinaigrette 98
sesame seeds 188
  fried eggplant with 178
  sesame chicken salad 118
  sesame tempura 78
sheer berenj 190
sherbet, sour cherry 192

shrimp, dried 156
shrimp paste 156
Sichuan chicken dumplings 100
Sichuan peppered beef 171
Sichuan spicy pickled
  cucumber 152
soups: miso soup with seven-spice
    chicken 97
  Nonya pork, shrimp, and crab
    ball soup 113
  Singapore coconut laksa 112
sour cherry sherbet 192
South Indian mango pickle 132
soy sauce 42–3
soy products 42–3
spare ribs, Chinese barbecue 25
spice blends 68–9
spices 206–7
split peas *see* peas, split
scallions: Laotian spice-
    pickled 168
  scallion and chive flower
    rolls 110
  scallion pancakes 61
spring rolls, shrimp and chive 73
squid: fried squid flowers with
    ginger and spices 58
Sri Lankan smoky eggplant dip 151
star anise 206
stock, dashi 97
suk ju 21
Sumatran eggplant sambal 89
Sumatran duck sate 51
sweet corn fritters, curried 70

T
tamari 43
tamarind: tamarind beef with
    peanuts 180
  tamarind fried shrimp 154
  tamarind sharbat 192
tamatar chatni 179
taruang balado 89
taugeh masak kerang 94
taukwa goreng 137
tempura, sesame 78
Thai curry pastes 69

tod man khao phad 70
tofu 43
tomatoes: spiced stuffed
    eggplant 165
  tomato chutney with green
    chile 179
trai me thit bo 180
tuna with ginger 121
Turkish zucchini fritters 64
turmeric 29
  Burmese turmeric fishcakes 80

U
urad dal: Keralan spiced chickpea
    and lentil dumplings 56

V
vaday 56
Vietnamese mint 139
Vietnamese peanut dipping
    sauce 153
vinaigrette, sesame and ginger 98
vinegar: black vinegar dipping
    sauce 122

W
wafers, crisp peanut 65
watermelon with lime, salt, and
    pepper 195
wonton wrappers: mushroom
    pot-stickers 107
  pork and cabbage dumplings 75
  steamed shrimp wontons 98

Y
yam som tam 144
yard-long beans: spicy green beans
    with chile 30
yogurt: spiced yogurt 82
  yogurt and pistachio cake 187
  yogurt and mint drink 209
yoogurtlu samfistigi kek 187

Z
zard choba pakora 67
zarda pilau 104
zucchini fritters, Turkish 64

Acknowledgments

Author's acknowledgment

Thank you to Mary-Clare Jerram, Carl Raymond, and Monika Schlitzer for seeing the potential in my writing; to Borra Garson and Lauren Davies at Deborah McKenna Ltd. Thank you to Dawn Henderson, Siobhán O'Connor, Susan Downing, and Simon Daley and the fantastic teams at DK in London, New York, and Germany. To everyone at Penguin in Australia for their help and support.

Thank you to Lisa Linder, and her assistant Julia Kepinska, for capturing the true essence of my food on film, and to Alice Hart for styling the food so beautifully.

Huge appreciation to the people from around the world who so generously helped in my pursuit of this book. First, Heather Paterson who makes my life work. To Tim Kemp for the fantastic opportunities in London and New York. In Malta, big thanks to Michael Zammit Tobana, owner of the Fortina Spa Resort; to the chefs at Taste, at the Fortina, who cook my food so well.

To the great cooks who have inspired me: Rose Gray and Ruth Rogers at the River Café, Rick Stein, Loyd Grossman, Peter Doyle from Est in Sydney, David Thompson.

To Tim Lee and Ashley Huntington, for keeping the debate on food wide open; Bernie Plaisted, for being my best man in the kitchen; Danielle and Rafael Fox Brinner, Kifah Arif, JJ Holland, Charlie Mash, Sarah Rowden, Clare Kelly, Birgit Erath, and Celia Brooks Brown. Thank you to the people who support my career: Chantal Rutherford Brown, the Cutting Edge School of Food and Wine, Books for Cooks, Susan Pieterse, Tertia Goodwin, everyone at Leiths, Liz Trigg, Toby Peters, Peter Durose,

Helen Chislet, Jaimin and Amandip Kotecha, Hugh and Celina Arnold, Gail Arnold and Howard Crump.

To Tasting Australia, Matt Maddocks, Wye Yap, Peter Harman, Susan Foster, Chris Pinzone, and everyone in Sydney. To Debbie Wallen, Annette Peters, Helena Fleming, Caroline Crumby at Marks & Spencer. To all the chefs and friends who make it so much fun. This book is for you.

Publisher's acknowledgment

Dorling Kindersley would like to thank Simon Daley and Siobhán O'Connor for being a joy to work with when the pressure is on, Andrew Roff for extra editorial assistance and Hilary Bird for producing the index.

Picture credits

The publisher would like to thank the following for their kind permission to reproduce their photographs:

Alamy Images: Melvyn Longhurst 212; Jon Arnold: 37, 108; Corbis: Krishnendu Halder/Reuters 146; Getty Images: Neil Emmerson 14; Frans Lemmens 199; David Noton 82; Anthony Plummer 166; Hugh Sitton 167; Keren Su 54, 116; VEER Steven Puetzer 126; Jochem D Wijnands 76; Lonely Planet Images: John Banagan 127; Photolibrary: Botanica 182; Photoshot: Joan Swinnerton 109; Rex Features: 36; Robert Harding Picture Library: Yadid Levy 198; Still Pictures: M. Lohmann 77

All other images © Dorling Kindersley
For further information see: www.dkimages.com